Creative Therapy
with
Children & Adolescents

Publisher's Note

This publication is designed to provide accurate and authoritative information in regard to the subject matter covered. It is sold with the understanding that the publisher is not engaged in rendering psychological, medical, or other professional service.

Books in The Practical Therapist Series® *present authoritative answers to the question, "What-do-I-do-now-and-how-do-I-do-it?" in the practice of psychotherapy, bringing the wisdom and experience of expert mentors to the practicing therapist. A book, however, is no substitute for thorough professional training and adherence to ethical and legal standards. At minimum:*

- *The practitioner must be qualified to practice psychotherapy.*

- *Clients participate in psychotherapy only with informed consent.*

- *The practitioner must not "guarantee" a specific outcome.*

— Robert E. Alberti, Ph.D., Publisher

Other Titles in The Practical Therapist Series®

Integrative Brief Therapy

Meditative Therapy

Metaphor in Psychotherapy

Rational Emotive Behavior Therapy

Creative Therapy
with
Children & Adolescents
A British Psychological Society Book

Angela Hobday, M. Sc. (Clin. Psych.)
Kate Ollier, M. Psych.

The Practical Therapist Series™

Impact Publishers, Inc.
ATASCADERO, CALIFORNIA 93423-6016

Impact Publishers and colophon are registered trademarks of Impact Publishers, Inc.

ATTENTION ORGANIZATIONS AND CORPORATIONS:
This book is available at quantity discounts on bulk purchases for educational, business, or sales promotional use. For further information, please contact Impact Publishers, P.O. Box 6016, Atascadero, CA 93423-6016 (Phone: 1-800-246-7228).

Library of Congress Cataloging-in-Publication Data

Hobday, Angela.
    Creative therapy with children & adolescents   /   Angela Hobday, Kate Ollier.
        p.   cm. -- (Practical therapist series)
    "A British Psychological Society book."
    Includes bibliographical references and index.
    ISBN 1-886230-19-6
    1. Child psychotherapy. 2. Arts--Therapeutic use. 3. Creation (Literary, artistic, etc.) -- Therapeutic use.   I. Ollier, Kate. II. Title.   III. Series.
RJ505.C63H63 1999
618.92'8914--dc21   99-17409
                                                      CIP

Cover design by Sharon Schnare, San Luis Obispo, California
Printed in the United States of America on acid-free paper
Published by **Impact Publishers, Inc.**
POST OFFICE BOX 6016
ATASCADERO, CALIFORNIA 93423-6016
www.impactpublishers.com

Contents

98425

❖ ## Chapter 10   *Reviewing Progress*   143

List of Illustrations

Foreword

Children are not miniature adults. So too, not all children are alike. Just as children vary in age, sex, and social circumstance, so they vary in their characteristic ways of thinking, feeling, and behaving. In conducting therapy with children, it is frequently necessary to adapt our treatments to characteristics of the individual child. In particular, it is necessary to adjust our therapy to the developmental level of the child and to meet children at their developmental level – cognitively, socially, and emotionally. However, this is easier said than done. All too frequently, we approach the treatment of children as if they were cut out of the same cloth or "cookie mold," and ignore important developmental and contextual aspects of the individual children with whom we are working. Such practice is likely to result in the children and their families being unhappy with treatment and, in many instances, to treatment being boring, if not ineffective as well. In this era of accountability and empirically supported treatments, we must do more to establish truly developmentally appropriate treatments that are also highly efficacious. The task is a difficult one, however.

In this compendium of creative activities for use with children and adolescents, the authors present us with a host of therapeutic actions to make our task of defining and using developmentally appropriate treatment strategies somewhat easier. The suggested games and activities are intuitively appealing and developmentally sensitive, having been developed on the front line of the authors' own clinical practice. They have not been more widely studied, at least as of yet, to prove that they enhance treatment outcomes. That work remains to be done. Of importance, however, Angela Hobday and Kate Ollier have provided us with grist for the therapeutic mill, and it will be up to us to evaluate use of these activities and to determine their empirical value.

This collection of creative activities has something for therapists of all theoretical persuasions and for children of all ages, and each therapist will likely find their own favorite activities. As a cognitive-behavior therapist, I found myself attracted to several activities, including "Spirals" (p. 69), "Shuddering Snakes and Likeable Ladders" (p. 80), "Clear Thinking" (p. 92), "Self-Talk" (p. 101), and "The Battle" (p. 89), to mention a few. With such attractive labels, the reader can begin to imagine the creativity and clinical acumen that went into the development of these varied and engaging activities.

One word of caution. In their Introduction, Hobday and Ollier warn us not to become totally reliant on this book. They assert that creative therapy and interesting activities will not resolve the child's problems unless your whole therapeutic approach is based on good foundations. I concur completely. This book should be viewed as a resource, nothing more and nothing less. My bet is that it will likely enhance empirically supported treatments, not replace them.

Thomas H. Ollendick, Ph.D.
Child Study Center
Department of Psychology
Virginia Polytechnic Institute and State University
Blacksburg, Virginia 24061

Acknowledgments

Thank you to our families for their patience and endurance. We are grateful to Ian and Jonathan for rescuing us with computing skills, and to Ken and Steph for proofreading. Thank you also to Beth, Josiah, and Eliza for helping us with the drawings, and to Zoë for being such a good baby while we worked. Finally, we are grateful to all the children on our caseloads whose individuality has sparked our creativity.

Introduction

C reative therapy with children and adolescents can be very elusive. Perhaps that is why clinical psychologists in training with us have been delighted (and sometimes relieved) to find our files of activities for use with children. We have found that many other professionals, including social workers, counselors, health visitors, and teachers, have also been interested in them. We use them frequently in our work, constantly adapting them to new children or circumstances. The children enjoy using them, so they begin to open up and work on their problems in a new way. The therapist or child worker usually has some fun too; using activities like these can spark ideas and lead to more creative therapy.

The activities in this book have been developed over several years, mostly out of necessity when children have found it difficult to discuss their problems or their feelings. They range from very simple ideas (which may well have already occurred to experienced therapists) to more complicated, innovative activities. While the versions presented in this book have all been designed by us, the inspiration has sometimes come from other sources (for example, some readers may recognize that "The Conquering Soldier" (Chapter 6, p. 94) is based on a very old bestseller!).

The general aim of this book is to encourage creativity in therapy and to assist in talking with children to facilitate change. The resources cover a wide variety of topics and include individual work with children and activities for families. A few of the resources are also useful in a group setting. The activities have been designed to be used as therapeutic tools to aid a variety of approaches, tailored to an individual child's needs. They are to be used in conjunction with assessing and treating through other means, for example, interviewing of caregivers, or with well-documented psychological approaches such as cognitive-behavioral therapy.

Throughout the North American edition of the book we have used the word "caregiver" to describe anyone who has care of the child or adolescent, whether it be a parent, grandparent, or other caregiver. This is for ease of reading. All the activities can be adjusted for girls or boys. If you follow the rule of adapting the material to the child, you will find that most of the activities can be used with a child who has reached the correct developmental stage.

❖ *Therapeutic Approach*

Our work as clinical psychologists is mainly based on cognitive therapy and constructive behavioral techniques, although we do borrow from other approaches (such as family therapy) to suit the needs of the child or family. A creative therapist should be able to mold many of the activities to whichever therapeutic approach he or she may be using.

You will see that rewards feature strongly in the book. Some caregivers resist rewarding because they do not want to "bribe" their children. We remind them that *bribes* are for doing wrong, whereas *rewards* are earned for working hard. Once given, rewards should never be taken away — not even on star charts. If children do not earn stars, they should not be punished or confused by being given black marks or black stars. The aim is to move children forward in a positive, constructive way to help them feel good about themselves.

❖ *How to Use This Book*

Each activity has been categorized according to the child's needs or the purpose of the activity, and grouped under the chapter headings. As a supplement to aid you in your initial assessment you can use items from the "Getting to Know You" section to begin to understand the problems of the child or family. Obviously, you also will need to know family details, the child's history, any trauma within the family, the caregiver's definition of the problem (as well as the child's), the caregiver's perception of the cause of the problem, and any attempted solutions. Only when you have a full understanding of what is going on will you be able to select an appropriate therapeutic approach and use these resources to supplement it. The assessment is also a good time to build rapport and give the family information about the services you offer.

From your initial assessment it should be possible to have an hypothesis about the cause of the child's problem. Using this as a basis for your therapy, decide on how you will help to effect change. The therapeutic approach you take will obviously depend on your particular skills as well as on the needs of the child and family. Work out your aims for therapy (for example, to teach anxiety management skills), and plan your sessions accordingly. Be prepared to be flexible and responsive to the child's level of ability and his own pace. Like all good stories, your therapy will need a beginning, a middle, and an end — the beginning being the assessment, the middle the ongoing therapy, and the end the review of progress. All of these parts are equally important.

Once you have begun to understand the cause of the difficulties and have a plan for how to approach them, you can use the chapter headings, or the index, to find appropriate activities from this book. The aim of each activity is clearly set out to help you to decide. As a general rule, start with the simplest activity for the child to understand, or the one that has the least emotional content, while you continue to build your rapport with the child.

It is hoped that you will use the activities as a jumping off point to begin to design your own. Try to adapt the tasks to the child's own likes and dislikes, for example, "The Battle" (Chapter 6, p. 89) may work better as a soccer match for a soccer-crazy ten-year-old. Some activities have variations. When you use these, be sure to read the instructions for the basic activity, because any instructions which are in common only appear in the main description under

"Method." At the end of each activity you will find a list of other activities which may be appropriate for similar problems.

As you proceed through the therapy you have planned for the child and family, you will gain more information. Use this new information to reassess the direction you are taking, and check to see if you are still using the best approach to effect change. Keep a record of changes made and review this regularly against your original assessment. Adjust your choice of activities to suit the child's needs as you proceed.

Finally, review the progress you have made. You will find the activities in Chapter 10 useful for this purpose. There are other activities in the book which can be adapted for review purposes and these are referenced in that chapter. It can be useful to repeat some of the initial assessment activities you have already used with the child to ascertain change. If you have adapted an activity to better suit a child, remember to use your adapted version again if you are assessing change.

❖ *Age and Child Development*

Each resource has an approximate age range indicated, but this will depend on the ability of the child. Use the age range as a guide only and note that many of the variations cater to older or younger children. The following guide to the relevant developmental stages may help you to judge whether the child you are working with can manage the task you present. (For a more comprehensive description of developmental stages, see Fahlberg, 1994, Chapter 2). All children are different, so the guide only indicates roughly what children are usually like within the ages described.

Relevant information regarding emotional development is included to assist you in helping caregivers to understand their children's feelings and behavior.

Birth–3 years

Children remain very dependent on their caregivers and have not fully developed language skills. Therapy with this age group is generally achieved through the training and educating of their caregivers, and therapy with such young children alone is relatively rare, except in cases of abuse/neglect or family problems where the child may provide information through disclosure. The activities in this book require interaction beyond the ability of this age group.

3–4 years

Most children of this age will have a vocabulary of between 1000–1500 words so they will be beginning to understand and answer comprehensive questions. They increasingly use words, instead of temper tantrums, to show their independence. Their level of communication and understanding means that they can make simple bargains, and can usually take turns. They enjoy simple games where they can use these skills. Be aware in therapy that children of this age seek to please, and thus may not appreciate the need to be honest.

Three- to four-year-olds are usually able to comprehend simple emotions such as "happy," "sad," and "angry," but may need to be given examples such as "have a temper tantrum" for angry. They are starting to share and can play in a group with others. Although they may have some separation difficulties as they start preschool, they can usually settle down and become confident in such surroundings. In the clinic setting, children of this age may want an older sibling or one of their parents in the room for added security.

4–5 years

Most four- to five-year-olds have extended their language to talk about the meanings of words. They can follow a two- or three-stage command, such as "Pick up your toys, put them in the box, and put on the lid." They can understand opposites and use questions extensively. Control is an issue for many children as they now start seeking to please themselves, and this can lead to them being argumentative. Imagination is important at this age and children also enjoy humor in play, although they cannot necessarily understand or tell jokes successfully. They may still tell fanciful stories.

Once children have begun school their experiences broaden and for a while they may be struggling to cope with all the change. This can lead to some difficult behavior, including being bossy and physically aggressive.

6–8 years

By the age of six, children will be very active. It is a wiggly sort of age, with increased frustration and sometimes children regress to younger behavior, including aggression and temper tantrums. Six-year-olds seem to swing from one end of the emotional scale to the other. They show enthusiasm at starting tasks but may have difficulty sticking to them without the encouragement of an adult. As they still want physical closeness, many children may revert to needing a cuddly toy or sucking a thumb, even if this has been outgrown once. Taking things that belong to others is fairly normal and children commonly "find" small items at school. They may call people names and tend to be verbally aggressive. In their general exploration of the world and how it works, they are sometimes cruel to animals. Response to praise is good which means that reward systems are likely to be effective. Generally, children of this age will understand your therapy and be able to follow a program.

Concentration generally improves by age seven and this means children can be more involved in the preparation and running of therapy programs. They may become engrossed in activities as they learn to concentrate better, giving adults the impression that they are being ignored. Children may still be forgetful and need to rely on adults. Being able to handle strong feelings is still difficult for seven-year-olds, who often end up fighting to resolve conflict or reduce tension. Children of this age cannot discuss how they feel while they are still upset, but may be able to later. They are usually poor at losing games and will sometimes cheat. However, they are beginning to develop a sense of fair play.

Seven-year-olds are able to understand another person's point of view (if this is explained to them) so they can see how their own actions affect others. This is usually the youngest age for using activities that need this skill of seeing how others react, such as "Escape Routes" (see p. 97).

Eight-year-old children may appear more settled in many ways. They can be happy, cheeky and boastful, and may be conscientious in their work with you. Usually they can work well in groups, although they may criticize others but be upset if they lose face. Children this age can usually begin to understand the process of time and its relevance to themselves. It is the earliest age at which activities like "Past, Present, Future" (p. 145) may be relevant. As eight-year-olds are becoming more skilled at dealing with hurt, they are less likely to respond with their fists. They are generally becoming more independent.

9–10 years

By nine years of age, children are beginning to plan ahead, which leads to hobbies such as collecting. They are less interested in fantasy games. They will respond to peer pressure and can work cooperatively in a group setting, although, because they prefer the company of their own sex, mixed groups can be hard work. A rising interest in activities such as sport may still be hampered by their wish to please their peers, rather than win. Nine-year-olds tend to respond to feelings of guilt and do not need to be told off to recognize right from wrong. They enjoy some responsibilities which can be useful for therapy. They can by now process information to use it in different situations. This means that in therapy they will be able to recognize new circumstances where a freshly learned behavior will apply.

Friendships are of great importance to most ten-year-olds and may become of greater relevance to children than their own family. The sex difference widens as girls mature more quickly and look down on the boys. However, children of this age will still enjoy family outings, especially if they can take a friend. By this age, life begins to have meaning and they can enjoy working together with a therapist.

11–13 years

During adolescence the child will need to begin to take on some adult values, but may still be expected to behave as a child. Young adolescents may vary greatly in the way they behave, and some of that variation will be linked to their physical development. They will be relying on themselves for control, rather than on an adult, but in many ways are not ready for this. They are typically fairly argumentative as they begin to form their own ideas and identities.

Eleven-year-olds may appear quite emotionally unstable, becoming suddenly angry or laughing hysterically. They may express anger through damaging property (especially bedroom doors) or even hitting others. In fact, young people in this age group are typically not very good at taking care of themselves or their possessions. Their rooms may be untidy with even their favorite clothes strewn about the floor. They are tired, but hate going to bed and dislike getting up. However, they are usually better at school than at home, sometimes enjoying competing with others. By now young adolescents are becoming more logical in their thinking and this will extend to matters outside their direct experience.

By twelve years of age there may be a certain amount of settling down so that the adolescent appears more eager to please. School can be very important to this age group as they begin to work more independently and become involved in discussions. Some of the extremes apparent at age eleven are now evident in other ways, so that the twelve-year-old may seem very enthusiastic about ideas or hate them. There is an increased interest in the opposite sex although "going out" with someone commonly involves no actual outings! A twelve-year-old who becomes angry may still use physical ways to demonstrate the anger despite being capable of verbal self-assertion.

As adolescents reach thirteen years they may become more introspective. This is a moody, sulky age as teenagers adjust to a new view of themselves, which may involve a lot of time in front of a mirror. This age group may be very keen not to be identified with their parents, and are usually very argumentative even about straightforward facts. Their anger may turn to tears (which they will find embarrassing), therefore, they are likely to sulk and storm out of the room before they reach this point. However, they are increasing in concentration, self-control, and the ability to organize themselves. It is important in therapy that the young teenager feels a sense of control over what is going on, and working together will improve chances of the program being considered valid and worthy of effort. Therefore, it is vital to work hard to fully engage a person of this age.

14–16 years

As children proceed through adolescence they are likely to have fewer specific fears, but more worries, which may be associated with school and the future. This is especially true of this age group with the pressure of school exams. Fourteen-year-olds appear more outgoing and generally enjoy life better. They seem friendly and responsible, especially to those outside the family. Even with their parents, relationships are less conflicting when parents are able to give them age-appropriate responsibility. Where there is conflict with parents or others, fourteen-year-olds are likely to resort to sarcasm, swearing or name calling, often under their breath. There may be a surge of aggressive impulses but it is also a time of increasing self-control. It helps greatly that the fourteen-year-old is becoming more objective and able to see another's point of view.

The peer group is very important and teenagers may want to spend many hours on the telephone, which gives them more time with friends, and also the chance to flirt with a member of the opposite sex with no risk of immediate consequences.

Fifteen-year-olds seem to lose some of their enthusiasm and become rather apathetic and indifferent. In actual fact they are going through another stage of introspection. There are life choices and decisions to be made and so naturally, adolescents are concentrating on sorting out their own thoughts, feelings, and opinions. There may be an increased tolerance of others at this age as teenagers become more sure of their own beliefs and values.

By the time adolescents reach sixteen they have generally become more self-reliant with a sense of direction. They should be less sensitive to criticism or advice and more capable in many spheres of life. By now they will have become more socially skilled and will know how to resolve conflicts successfully. If they have been given the right opportunities they should have sufficient life skills to look after themselves independently. For adolescents of this age, therapy is best presented as a series of choices to be made, so that they have the responsibility of direction. For example, provide them with information and possible options, and let them look at the costs and benefits of each.

Many adolescents enjoy looking toward their future and examining their own thoughts, which makes activities like "Past, Present, Future" (p. 145) very suitable for this age group.

❖ *Length of Activity*

It has not been possible to give the length of time that each activity will take, as this varies with the individual child and on your own approach in using the material. However, we have tried to indicate where an activity will take much longer than one session. Always allow plenty of time for an activity, as children will feel pushed aside if you stop it before it is completed. It is better to start it early on in the session if you are unsure of the child's rate of working.

Once you have used several activities with a child, you will be able to judge the time you will need. If you ever do run out of time, try to reach a natural breakpoint in the activity and tell the child clearly what you will be doing next time you meet to complete it. Make sure you make a note of this so that the child is not disappointed. Generally, it is a good rule not to attempt to use more than one activity per session, unless you are reviewing progress from a previous session.

❖ *Materials*

All the illustrations, worksheets, and appendices within this book are copyright-free. However, you may find that you need to enlarge some of the material for ease of use. Please note that the rest of the material in this book remains subject to usual copyright restrictions.

Other items required are indicated for each activity — but you may be able to use alternative materials you have at hand. Experienced therapists will know the importance of choosing the right materials. For example:

- Children of up to about eleven or twelve years generally enjoy using colored paper, colored pencils, and marking pens. Make sure you have some marking pens fine enough for writing as well as for drawing.
- Older children may prefer using more adult pens with white paper.
- Children take pride in their work and like to keep it in their own special folder which they can take home and bring back to sessions (but do make photocopies for your clinical file).
- Children like to help with photocopying (if possible) so that they know what happens to their work.
- For some activities, you will need safety scissors, thin card stock and paste (or a gluestick), counters, and dice.
- Simple glove puppets are useful for role-play and some of the activities in this book. Children like it if the puppets have names.
- Play-Doh™ or modeling clay is useful for some activities.

❖ The Setting

You may have no control over where you see the child and family, but it is important to make it as comfortable as possible, especially for the younger age group. Younger children like surroundings with soft toys and a few puzzles, building bricks, toy cars, or a tea set to play with while you are talking to the caregivers. Even teenagers enjoy comfortable surroundings, but it is best to put away the toys. Leave a few items out that they may need. For example, the teddy bear cushion in our clinic is often picked up and hugged by teenage boys or girls as they talk about their feelings or difficult circumstances. Generally, over-sixes will draw in the same room while you are talking to the adults, but they may need regular input to keep them to task. Obviously, children with extreme anxiety, behavior, or attention problems will not settle down, and you may wish to ask the caregiver to bring another adult to sit with the child in the waiting area while you obtain the necessary background information. Similarly, if any information that the caregiver gives you is likely to be detrimental to the child, arrange a time to see the caregiver alone.

Children can settle to work more easily in a quiet room and with chairs and a table that are the right size for them. You will need to sit at the same level as they do, so make sure you have a suitable low chair. If there is no low table, over-fives can manage to sit on a standard chair at a regular sized table. It is best to sit by the side of the child, or on the adjacent side of the table (not opposite), so that you can both see the piece of work without too much turning of it this way and that.

When you are seeing a whole family, make sure you have enough chairs (at the same height as yours) and plenty of room. You may find it useful to have a few toys or a drawing area if there are younger children, but be careful not to exclude them from the therapy if you are using a family approach.

❖ *Format of Sessions*

Try to invite to your initial assessment the key family members (including stepfamily members if they live with the child). A minimum would be caregiver and child. Within each session it is important to offer time to the child alone, and this is usually when many of the activities in this book can be best used. At the end of each session, with the child's permission, give feedback to the caregiver (usually with the child present). Explain why you have done the task with the child, and encourage the child to tell the caregiver all about it. Together with the caregiver, decide on any homework tasks which will consolidate the work done during the session. Do not forget to review the homework at the beginning of the subsequent session.

❖ *Level of Prompting*

The level of prompting appropriate for the activities will depend on the ability and personality of the child. Within some of the instructions you will find we have indicated where further questioning of the child is needed, or how to elicit extra information. As a general rule, younger children will cope better with choosing between a few suggestions, while those around eight or nine will be able to manage prompts which ask for examples. Teenagers will usually respond to open-ended questions, so long as they are socially skilled and you have established good rapport.

❖ *General Tips for Working with Children*

Although every child is different and needs an individual approach, we have included some general observations and suggestions which may be useful:

- Some children will want to do the writing themselves, and others will want you to be their "secretary." It is best to offer them a choice.

- Remember that the resources are only useful when the child is having fun and is taking an active role. If the child is not interested, it is better to use an alternative activity.

- Let the child have as much control over the tasks as possible, for example, choosing colors.

- If children are anxious about working in front of you it will help them to participate if you do it *badly* first. For example, once you have drawn very basic stick men you will generally find they want to draw something a bit more exciting.

- Children have a right to confidentiality within legal bounds — discuss with them before talking to their parents about their work. Explain to children that they do not have to show their file of work to their parents, it is up to them.

- Making therapy fun will help to relax children so that they are more likely to open up to you.

- A few children's jokes up your sleeve may help (but make sure they are good, clean, fun and will not sound like something else by the time the children tell the jokes to their caregivers in their own unique way!).

- For filling in forms at home, involve children in marking boxes, applying stickers, and so on, whenever possible, so that they feel in control of the program.

- Always try to have your materials ready before the session, or at least within easy reach.

- Try to make a link between sessions by referring to a non-emotive item that the child raised in the previous session. For example, "How are the baby rabbits?"

❖ *A Word of Warning*

Do not become totally reliant on this book alone! Creative therapy and interesting activities will not resolve the problem unless your whole approach is based on good foundations. Therefore, remember to use your psychological training and approaches which have been scientifically tried and tested. The activities in this book are extra resources and will not turn you into a child therapist! In fact, it is your skills as a therapist which will turn these ideas into useful therapeutic tools.

— Angela Hobday and Kate Ollier

Getting To Know You

The activities in this section are designed to be used early on as part of the assessment process. As we explained in the Introduction, under "How to Use this Book," they are not meant to take the place of the initial interview because you will need to gain a wide range of information to be able to understand what is going on. Not only will these exercises help you to assess the situation, they will also help you to begin to establish rapport with the children and introduce them to the idea of talking about themselves and their difficulties.

❖ My World   Age: 4-11 years

Aim
To establish rapport, provide an opportunity for the child to practice talking about herself in a nonthreatening way, obtain information about the child as a person in her own right, and help the child to feel positive about herself. This should be done *before* tackling emotional problems.

Materials
Paper, marking pens and pencils, and perhaps a small round plate to draw around.

Method
Most seven-year-olds and over will be able to manage this version of the activity. Younger children will enjoy the variation (see p. 20).

Explain to the child that you will be doing a task together to help you to learn a little more about her. Ask her if she knows how to draw a world because you may draw something a bit like that. If she does not seem to understand, she may not manage the task, so move to the variation of this activity instead with the explanation that you have thought of something better to do.

If the child does seem able to cope with the activity, write (or ask her to write) the heading "My World by —" and ask her to write in her name. Then ask the child to draw (or draw it yourself) a large circle on the paper, describing it as a world. Let her put stars around the outside and maybe a moon or a rocket. Talk to the child about how she has her own world — people she likes to be with, things she likes to do, and so on. Encourage her to tell you about her world by asking her about herself. Try to keep to positives for this initial task. Examples of some useful questions would be:

- What is your favorite food?
- Who is your best friend?
- What do you like to do after school?
- What pets do you have?
- What are you good at?
- What are your favorite clothes?
- What television program do you like watching?
- Where do you like to go at weekends/holidays?

Try to adapt your questions to the child, picking up on your rapidly increasing knowledge of her to frame your questions. For example, if you find she likes soccer, your next question could be about the team she supports. As the child answers you, put her answers in the "world" and encourage her to put an "island" around each one. When you have finished, she may wish to complete the picture by coloring in the sea and filling in other details (see the example, "My World by Jos," p. 20).

Talk about the drawing with her, explaining that all the separate things (the islands) make up the whole (the world). Just as the world is unique, so too is she.

Our example, which was produced by a seven-year-old boy, only contains five pieces of information, and this amount may be all a child is prepared to volunteer in one sitting. However, the therapist will have been able to build on this with questions such as "Who is Simon?" and "Are there other subjects you like in school?" Doing the task has also given other information about the child, for example, she may have good drawing skills and be able to concentrate well on a task in a one-to-one situation. Altogether, the therapist had gained access to quite a large amount of information which could be fed back to the child to illustrate her uniqueness.

Variation

I Am...

A simpler task for a younger or less able child does not use the idea of a world. Instead, ask the child to draw a picture of herself in the middle of a piece of paper and write "I AM—" with the child's name on the top (see p. 21). (If she cannot manage this, then you could do the drawing.) Explain that this exercise is to see what sort of person she is, what she likes, and so on, and to find out all about her. Give her a few ideas, by asking similar questions to those suggested in "My World" and write these all around the drawing. Again, try to keep this positive, and help the child who has low self-esteem to find some positive attributes.

Our example has given useful insights into the life and interests of a five-year-old girl. In this case she wanted to draw all the pictures, but asked for some help with the writing. Be prepared to respond to the needs and abilities of the child, perhaps by adding your own illustrations if the child wants this.

See also:

- Feelwheel (p. 31)
- Good Things about Me (p. 131)
- Happy, Sad, Angry (p. 23)
- I Believe (p. 138)
- Importance Jars (p. 133)

my World by Jos.

I am Eliza

My favorite
color is
purple

I like
writing at
school

I like
going
to my
friends

my brother
is Jos

My favorite
food is
macaroni
and cheese

I go to
ballet

my best
friend is
HOlly

I like
milk

❖ *Sentence Completion   Age: 4 years and up*

Aim
To assess the child's way of thinking about specific issues. Can be used to assist disclosure by encouraging the child to talk about an issue.

Materials
Paper, marking pens. A notebook can be used instead of loose paper.

Method
This activity is particularly useful with children who are very shy and find eye contact difficult. Try to create a game-like atmosphere by talking about taking turns to write and choosing which color pen you will each have. You then write the beginning of a sentence and the child completes it either by writing or telling the end. You should start off fairly gently; for example, "One thing that makes me happy is...," moving to more in-depth questions as the child gets used to the idea and "warms up."

Be alert to the child's non-verbal response to the questions. If he looks as if he is finding a particular subject matter difficult you may need to move on to a safer area for a while, to help him relax. You must judge the pace, and remember to end on a happier sentence. Go through the responses with the child afterwards, inviting him to expand on any areas where you need more information.

Variation
A Person Like Me
This activity can be included in a book which you write together, where a fictional character goes through a similar experience to the child. The child fills in the sentences, for example, how he felt, whom he could talk to, and how he felt after talking about it. End the book on a positive note.

See also:
- Feelwheel (p. 31)
- Happy, Sad, Angry (p. 23)

❖ *Happy, Sad, Angry   Age: 5-14 years*

Aim
To introduce talking about feelings, and to give permission to have feelings such as anger or sadness. This provides an indirect way for the child to raise issues of emotional importance and allows the child to discuss emotional feelings without having to cope with the task of talking directly to the therapist.

Materials
Marking pens and paper.

Method
Ask younger children, or those who have already shown they enjoy artwork, to draw three different faces (labeled "Happy," "Sad," "Angry"). Encourage the child to draw the pictures fairly small and evenly spaced across the page so that writing can be fitted in above or below each one. However, if all the pictures end up on one side, draw shapes or thought bubbles to link the pictures and writing (see example, p. 24). Then, ask her about what makes her feel this way — for younger children, ask them "When do you feel happy?" and so on. For older children, the task can be more abstract, for example, "What makes you happy?" Start the task with the positive emotion (Happy), and discuss each example given. When the negative feelings have been discussed, bring the child back to the positive emotion for a happy ending.

In our example, doing the task has already given information about the split family situation and the fact that the child's father does not always keep contact visits. It also highlights the probability of a difficult relationship with the elder brother.

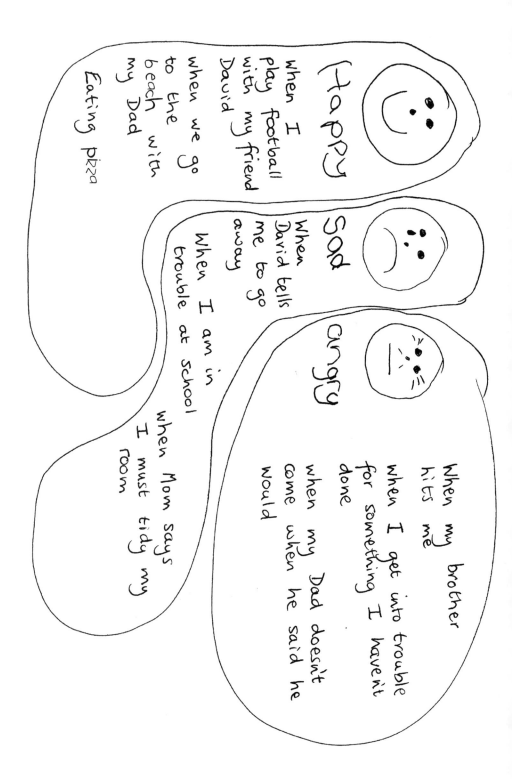

Happy

When I play football with my friend David my friend

When we go to the beach with my Dad

Eating pizza

Sad

When David tells me to go away

When I am in trouble at school

Angry

When my brother hits me

when I get into trouble for something I haven't done

when my Dad doesn't come when he said he would

when Mom says I must tidy my room

Variation

Happy, Worried, Confused

For anxious children, you can also use feelings like "Worried," "Embarrassed," "Confused," but limit the task to four emotions and have at least one positive emotion.

See also:

- Facemask (p. 27)
- Feelwheel (p. 31)
- Mood Scales (p. 30)
- My World (p. 17)

❖ *Reasons Why   Age: 5 years and up*

Aim

To help children recognize the reasons for their behavior and to promote honesty and understanding in talking about difficult subjects where children might think they are naughty. This will give you insight as to how to target your therapy.

Materials

Marking pens and paper. For the variation, two boxes (see template in Appendix I, p. 155) and index cards.

Method

Make up a list of possible reasons for a certain behavior, including some crazy, unlikely ones (see our list of examples of reasons for wetting the bed, p. 26). Go through them with the child, explaining each one carefully. Ask him to go through them with you again, letting you know which ones apply to him. Circle those which apply, and cross out the others. Leave some blank spaces for him to add any other reasons which he may have.

Once you have the list of reasons, praise the child for being able to talk about it. This task then leads well to an activity such as "Costs and Benefits" (see p. 56), which will open up the possibility of change.

Reasons Why I Wet the Bed

- Don't know that I've done it until I wake up.
- It's too warm and cozy in bed to get up.
- I'm too busy playing and I forget I have to go.
- I'm afraid to go on my own at night.
- There are no lights and I'm afraid of the dark.
- I like to swim in my bed.
- I like to get into trouble.
- Once I've started peeing I can't stop.
- I only do it when someone comes into my room.
- I like Mommy to give me a bath in the middle of the night.

Variation

List The Reason

Write out all the reasons on index cards. Have two shoeboxes (see the template in Appendix I, p. 155) and mark one of them "No, not me" and the other "Yes, me." Let the child place each card in the appropriate box. Then take out all the cards from "Yes, me" and arrange them in order, with the child saying which is the main reason for her behavior.

See also:

- Costs and Benefits (p. 56)
- The Wall (p. 51)
- Zoro Reaches the Mountain Top (p. 44)

Feelings

C hildren often have real difficulty talking about feelings. Teenagers in particular will sometimes shrug their shoulders at the suggestion that they may feel sad or really pleased about something. The following activities are designed to help both children and adolescents express feelings and to create a therapeutic environment within which it is easier to talk. It is also easier to avoid eye contact (which may feel very threatening for a client) when both client and therapist are focused on a task.

❖ Facemask   Age: 3–8 years

Aim
To help the child realize that people cover up feelings. Especially useful when a child is being bullied by another unhappy child.

Materials
Marking pens and paper. For variations, Play-doh™ or modeling clay, and index cards.

Method
Draw a face which is happy one way up, but sad (or scared) the other. You will need to cheat a bit with the frown to make sure it is a smile the other way up (see the example on p. 29). Show this to the child a few times, turning it around to show him how it works, and, depending on his age, perhaps let him have a try at drawing his own. Then, starting under the smiley face, write a suitable legend around the face, such as "Sometimes when

I smile I am really feeling sad inside." Try to put the words "smile" and "sad" immediately under the appropriate face. Discuss with the child all about covering up feelings, perhaps with reference to an incident in his own life when he or someone else pretended to be happy when they were really sad.

Variation
3-D Facemask
This an excellent activity for Play-doh™, but of course it is not possible to write on it in the same way, or to store it in a workbook, if you are keeping one. However, it could be made in a more three-dimensional manner in a lightweight modeling material, and stuck to a card.

See also:
- Happy, Sad, Angry (p. 23)
- Mood Scales (p. 30)

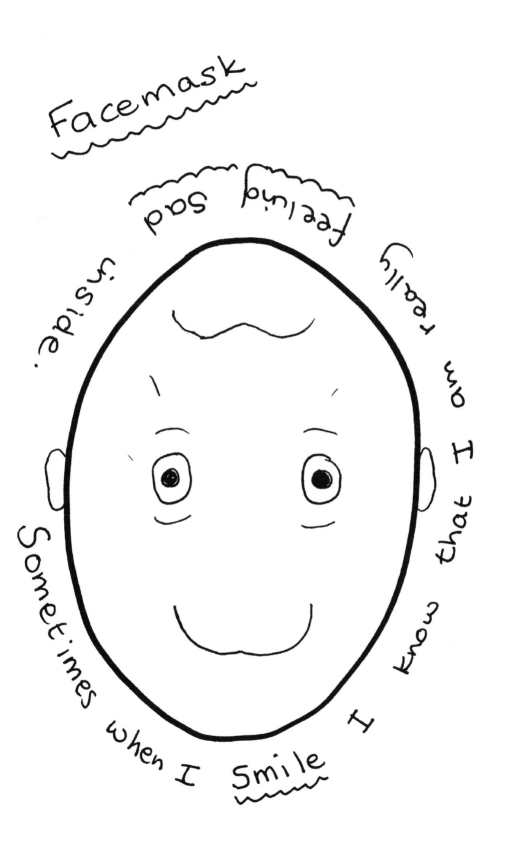

Facemask

Sometimes when I Smile I know that I am really feeling sad inside.

❖ *Mood Scales   Age: 6 years and up*

Aim

To assess a child's perception of self on a variety of potential problem areas. It aims to provide an easy, visually accessible means of assessment which can be used at various points throughout therapy to monitor progress.

Materials

Prepared worksheet (see Appendix II, p. 157) using paper, pens.

Method

Prepare the worksheet by drawing a number of horizontal lines of equal length on a page and writing along the top line a series of numbers from 0 to 6, equally distanced. Alternatively, put the numbers 0 to 6, equally spaced, along each line. At the left end of each line write the concept/feeling that is to be assessed (see sample scale in Appendix II, p. 157). Do not have more than ten concepts; probably less for younger children. Make sure you include any moods which your assessment interview has shown to be relevant. For example, if the child has anger difficulties, include "angry" as a measure. Over the "0" put the words "Not at all" and over the "6" write "Very much so." At this stage, make copies of the worksheet to re-use with the child at a later date.

To use the worksheet, ask the child to circle on each line the number which reflects the extent to which she felt each of the concepts through the week. Make sure she understands how to use the scale. Go through her responses, asking her to elaborate on each one (why she feels this way, what changes it, how long she has felt this way, and so on).

Variation
Mood Faces
For younger children use a smaller number of topics and use faces rather than numbers which can go from looking very sad, to neutral, to very happy. Use a 5- or 3-point scale with the younger age-group.

See also:
- Feelwheel (p. 31)
- Happy, Sad, Angry (p. 23)

❖ *Feelwheel   Age: 7 years and up*

Aim
To elicit feelings related to individual circumstances or situations, to help the client to recognize these feelings, and lead to discussion about how they affect his or her actions.

Materials
Marking pens and construction paper, split pin brass fastener, scissors.

Method
Cut a piece approximately one-inch wide from one end of the paper. Put this to one side. On the rest of the paper, draw a large circle and divide it into several pie sections. Explain to the child that each radius represents the spoke of a wheel. Label each section with a different emotion, making sure you cover a wide range. For example, choose from the following list: *excited, scared, proud, peaceful, confused, angry, sad, disappointed, happy, embarrassed, guilty, lonely.* (You may have others which are more relevant to the child or your assessment.) Limit the number of feelings according to the abilities of the child, that is, the younger the child, the fewer the sections. Explain what you are doing as you make the Feelwheel, encouraging the child to help and to contribute categories.

Make an arrow out of the other piece of construction paper which is wide enough for the fastener, and about two-thirds of the radius of the circle. Cut the arrow out and fix it to the center with a fastener.

For younger children. Discuss a situation (involving either the child or a fictional character) and ask her to choose how she/the character would feel by moving the arrow to point to the appropriate feeling. Start with situations which are not too close to the child's problem and gradually draw closer to her own difficulties.

For older children. Use as with younger children, but also ask the child to discuss situations when she has felt these emotions or witnessed them in someone else. The child may want to write down examples for each feeling.

The wheel can be used without an arrow, with the therapist or child pointing instead.

Variation
Feelings Pie
The Feelwheel can be drawn as a feelings pie, complete with pie crust (see illustration). Use in the same manner as the Feelwheel.

See also:
- Facemask (p. 27)
- Happy, Sad, Angry (p. 23)
- Mood Scales (p. 30)
- My World (p. 17)

My feelings pie
By Tracey

Happy
when I was chosen for volleyball by Alice

Excited
when Becky's coming

Angry
when my Mom tells me off

Calm
Don't know

Sad
when my cat Ginger died

Confused
when my Mom went into hospital

Nervous
when I went to my new School

Proud
that I got my swimming certificate for 100 meters

❖ *A Pocketful of Feelings*   *Age: 7 years and up*

Aim
To help the child recognize and talk about his feelings, linking them to incidents in his own life.

Materials
Two pieces of construction paper, scissors, marking pens, large envelope and glue.

Method
With one sheet of paper and the envelope, make a large paper pocket. You may wish to shape the top of the envelope and draw on stitching to make it more pocket-like. Glue the pocket onto the paper, and write on the title with the child's name. Take the other piece of paper and, with the child, make a list on it of a wide range of feelings (as in Feelwheel, p. 31). Keep the writing fairly small, so that each feeling can be cut out to drop into the pocket. Cut your list into strips and put them in the pocket. Take turns pulling out a feeling and talk about when the feelings arise, for example, "When do you feel sad?" This can lead to helping the child discuss specific incidents and how he felt at the time. You can then use your skills as a therapist to help the child to understand the feelings which arose, and perhaps to begin to realize how other people may also feel.

The pocket can also be used to talk about feelings of emptiness, if appropriate.

Note: Obviously, use discretion when discussing your own feelings, making sure they are not personal. Remember, this is the child's session so your examples should simply facilitate the child's expression and should not supply any personal information.

Variations

Boxful of Feelings

Instead of a pocket you could make a box (see the template in Appendix I, p. 155) for a "Boxful of Feelings." Use in the same way as the pocket.

Acting Out Feelings

For either of the versions you can use the cards for the child to role-play situations where the feelings arise. You could make it more of a game by asking them to act out something as if they are feeling what is on the card, for example, "Wash your face as if you are happy."

See also:

- Facemask (p. 27)
- Feelwheel (p. 31)
- Happy, Sad, Angry (p. 23)
- Mood Scales (p. 30)
- My World (p. 17)

❖ *Heartstrings   Age: 8 years and up*

Aim

To give insight into how children view significant others in their lives. This can lead to a discussion with the child as to why some people are less close to him than others.

Materials

Marking pens and paper.

Method

Draw a series of evenly spaced circles, one inside the other, the smallest being about two inches in diameter, and the largest about eight inches. Four are usually sufficient but you may need to add a further circle as the child progresses through the activity.

In the center of the smallest circle, draw a heart shape and let the child write his name inside it. Then explain to the child that this diagram will be for him to work out who feels close and important to him, or who he loves the most. Explain that the names of the people who are most important to him are to be written in the next circle closest to the heart. Then other people who are not quite so close go in the next circle, and so on (see example, p. 38). Some children will find it easier to work out a list of people first and then categorize them in this way. Discuss with the child his reason for putting people in certain positions.

This exercise has proved especially useful when children move between families, for example, into foster care, or live with a separated parent (as in the example). Children who feel torn between parents gain from standing back from the situation and sorting it out on paper. Be prepared for the child to make discoveries while doing this exercise, for example, suddenly realizing that he has stronger feelings for a stepfather than he has for his natural father. Let the child know that it is all right to be honest with you about his feelings.

Variations
My Heart, Your Heart
On certain occasions it may be useful to do the exercise twice, first, as in "Heartstrings," with the child saying how close other people feel to him. After this, the child decides where each of the significant people would place themselves in relation to the child. The two sets of circles may be very different. Discuss with the child why this is the case.

Family Heartstrings

This is best used by experienced family therapists as it is a very powerful exercise. The exercise is done as a family sculpture, with the child standing in the center, imagining the circles around him and saying how close the rest of the family need to go. It is especially important to follow this sculpture through with discussion about how those who are placed far away can move closer. Always end the exercise with the family saying nice things about each other or hugging, so that no one leaves the room feeling pushed away (a useful task here would be "51 Ways to Praise," p. 121).

See also:
- Draw a Family Doing Something Together (p. 115)
- Portions of Parenting (p. 126)
- Who's Who (p. 117)

Heartstrings

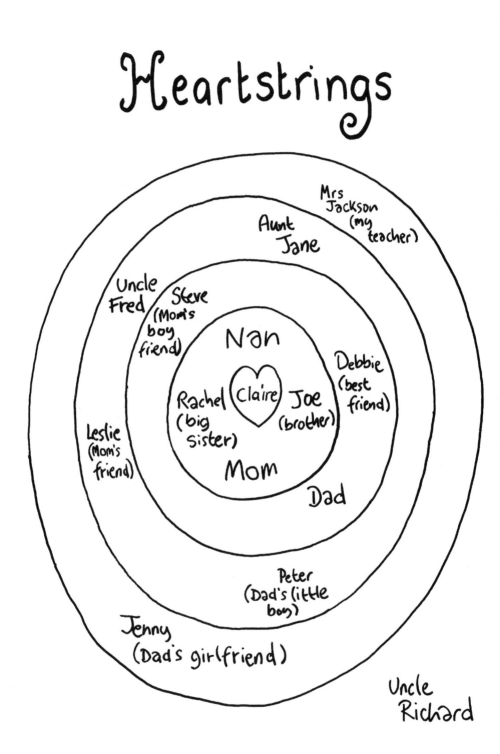

Increasing Motivation To Change

Asignificant factor in any successful program is being able to maintain the motivation required to keep a child working toward her goal. If a child is not interested, no program will succeed. The following activities cover a range of ways in which the interest of a child or adolescent can be maintained. They help to clarify goals, provide a structure for progress, and act to remind the child of how to get there. It should be noted that all these activities require follow-up after completion to ensure long–term success.

❖ Comfort Squares   Age: 3–12 years

Aim
To put a boundary on unwanted behavior which occurs on a regular basis, with a view to decreasing its frequency to zero. It makes a game out of putting a limit on behavior.

Materials
Index cards, marking pens

Method
First get a measure of how often the target behavior is happening. Decide (with caregivers and even the children themselves if appropriate) how often within an hour/day/week the behavior will initially be acceptable. For example, if after being put to bed a child comes downstairs to say goodnight around fifteen times each night, then twelve times might be the initial number — it has to be within relatively easy reach for the child to succeed.

Make a set of cardboard squares, which the child is to use as tokens, each square representing one occurrence of the target behavior. Label each token as appropriate, for example, "one token for going downstairs." Explain to the child that you will be working on doing the behavior less, and so from now on, she can only do it if she has a square to give Mom or Dad first. The child is given all of the squares at the beginning of the time frame, for example, when sent to bed, and is reminded that each time she performs the unwanted behavior, she will have to pay with one square. Once the squares are all gone, she can't do it anymore (during that time frame). Have caregivers be insistent (within reason!) on this last rule of the game.

Once the child is managing with the number of squares allowed, she receives a reward and the game is reviewed to reduce the number of squares — "Jennie, how many squares do you think you need these days?" "How about you try with nine?" As each goal is reached, the child is rewarded and then the number of token squares is reduced. Once you have got down to one, if necessary, increase the time frame, so that instead of one a night, it is one every Monday and Thursday, or one a week.

This task is obviously not suited to behaviors that are dangerous or which involve siblings (for example, fighting), where a zero tolerance level is to be expected, but it is very useful for behaviors which the child wants to work on and where the length of time taken to extinguish a behavior is not important. For example, we have found it to be successful with children working on the following problems:

- Getting out of bed after bedtime
- Collecting "useless" items (inability to throw away)
- Insisting on lots of stories being read each night
- Playing too many computer games
- Watching too many videos or the same one repeatedly.

Variation

That's My Limit

For older children you can simply set limit, such as "Phoning Mom six times a day," with the child keeping a record of the number. The principle is the same in that the limit is gradually reduced over time, at a pace which allows the child to feel in control.

See also:
- Staircase to Success (p. 49)
- Zoro Reaches the Mountain Top (p. 44)

❖ *A Child Called...   Age: 3–12 years*

Aim

To offer understanding of a child's behaviors and worries, and promote his coping skills. This is done through a personalized book, which can be read at home in between appointments. This activity will probably take more than one session.

Material

A project folder or paper and some sort of "spine" to hold the pages together, marking pens.

Method

Write and illustrate a personalized book for the child, which deals with the problem subject. The book should be about ten pages, with many drawings for younger children and more writing for older children. If the book is promoting positive behavior, use the child's name. However, if it is helping the child to acknowledge difficult feelings and assist him in coping, it may be easier for the child if you distance the book by using another name.

When writing the book, use the child's information to assist you. Keep the text simple and time efficient. Depending on the subject matter, you may want the child to help you write it, but make sure you direct it to a happy and positive (but realistic) ending. Sometimes it works well to discuss the text of the book on one occasion and have it typed up ready for the next session, when the child can illustrate it.

Once written and illustrated, ask the caregiver to read it with the child regularly (so long as the child is interested) between sessions. Review the child's progress in later sessions. The book may lose its appeal within a short period, but caregivers may want to reintroduce it at a later date if the child regresses.

The following example text ("Clever Joe," p. 43) is for a four-year-old boy who regularly woke his parents at night. He was unable to sleep in his parents' bed and the broken sleep led to behavior problems during the day. With the birth of another child imminent, the parents were anxious to help Joe resolve the problem.

See also:
- Best Achievements (p. 143)
- Past, Present, Future (p. 145)
- The Story So Far (p. 148)

Clever Joe

Once upon a time there was a little boy called Joe.
Joe lived with his Mommy and Daddy in a special house that had an upstairs and a downstairs.

Joe had his own room with his own toys and his own books and his own bed.

Sometimes Joe would wake up and wonder where his Mommy was. He would call out and she would give him a cuddle and sometimes he would try to go to sleep in his Mommy's bed.

But sometimes Joe would remember to be a really clever boy and go and sleep in his own bed.

Mommy had a baby in her tummy and it was getting bigger and bigger.

One day she went to the hospital because the baby was ready to be born.

Mommy stayed at the hospital for a few days, and Daddy and Joe had to look after themselves all by themselves.

Joe was very pleased to help his Daddy with cleaning and cooking and lots of playing.

Joe and Daddy made sure that the house was ready for when Mommy and Baby came home.

When Mommy was in the hospital, Joe showed Daddy that he could stay in his own bed all by himself.

Mommy and Baby came home from the hospital and Daddy was very pleased to tell Mommy what a clever boy Joe was because he stayed in his own bed.

Mommy said that Joe is a wonderful big brother for the Baby.

Joe helps Mommy lots of times now. And there are four special people living in his house.

> Mommy
> Daddy
> Baby... and...
> CLEVER JOE

❖ *Zoro Reaches the Mountain Top*   *Age: 4–10 years*

Aim
To provide a record sheet for progress over several weeks or sessions which allows for slips back and records overall progress. It is best used when some progress has already been made.

Materials
Colored paper, marking pens, pencil.

Method
Fold back approximately one inch of the right-hand side of the page (long sides vertical). With the child, draw a mountain which fills the rest of the page. In pencil, draw a path going up the mountain which crosses from side to side and has dips and bulges in it (see example, p. 45). The child may want to put trees, bushes, and rocks on the mountain, but don't let her put in more than two or three at this stage, as you may need to add them in later as part of the record. Talk to her generally about climbing mountains and about how mountaineers make bases where they stop for the night to pitch their tents. At each base they will put up their flagpoles. Explain that each session with you is like a base camp (or each alternate session if you are seeing them frequently or if progress is likely to be very slow). Fold out the edge and put a scale on it with goals; for example, for a nine-year-old child with nocturnal enuresis who could already achieve four dry beds per two-week period, the scale used was:

- Dry bed nearly every night
- Dry bed 13 nights out of 14
- Dry bed 10 nights out of 14
- Dry bed 8 nights out of 14
- Dry bed 6 nights out of 14
- Dry bed 5 nights out of 14
- Dry bed 4 nights out of 14

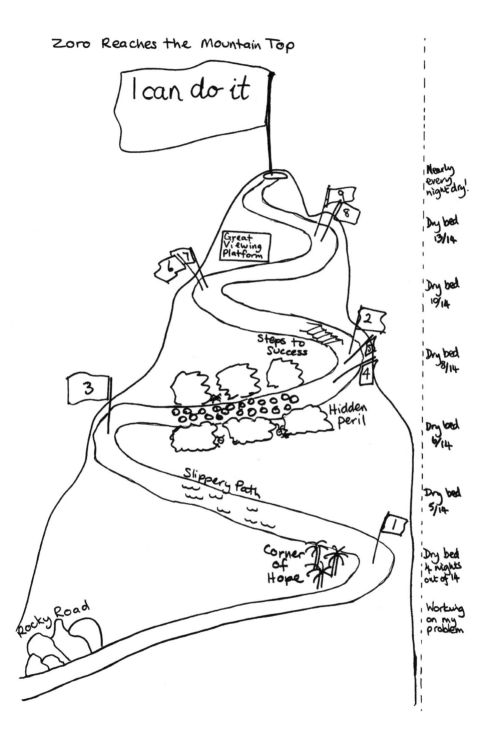

Always make the item at the top of your page to be near total success, but not absolute perfection. Allow for some mistakes, and explain to the caregivers that any child learning a new skill is likely to make some errors sometimes (and that mistakes must not be punished but seen as a new bit to learn).

As sessions progress, put a flag in the path at the appropriate level to indicate the progress the child has made. If she has gone backwards from the past session, let her draw some rocks in the way and discuss what has got in the way of progress since last time. You may wish to extend this aspect of the task by drawing a page of rocks with the problems named on each and then have a pickaxe by the side with solutions. Color in the path as the child progresses up the mountain, putting appropriate dips in the path if the child has regressed. Make sure sudden improvements are recorded as well. Put a date by the flag or by the scale as the child prefers, or number each flag and keep a note of the dates yourself. The scale can be folded away so that the child can hang the picture at home without embarrassment.

Once the mountain top is reached, celebrate the achievement and draw a flag on the top with a figure to represent the child. The child can keep the drawing as a reminder of a great achievement (but don't forget to also make a copy for the clinic file).

See also:
- Reasons Why (p. 25)
- Staircase to Success (p. 49)

❖ *Beat the Bell*   *Age: 4–14 years*

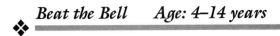

Aim
To speed up the completion of a task or set of tasks by providing a challenge which offers a meaningful reward. It is especially useful for children who dawdle over activities, such as eating a meal, in order to gain extra attention or because they are easily distracted. Progress will be monitored over several sessions.

Materials
For younger children you may want to use photos or pictures cut from magazines to depict each task. You will need an alarm clock, kitchen timer, or a bell (if the caregiver is able to keep an eagle eye on the time).

Method
Choose a task (such as putting his toys away or tidying his bedroom) or set of tasks (for example, getting ready for school) which the child must complete. Define specifically what counts as proper completion — getting ready for school has a number of tasks which must each be defined and have minimum quality standards, such as those described in the boxed example.

Getting Ready for School

- Eat breakfast sitting at the table.
- Brush teeth properly; put away the brush and toothpaste.
- Wash face clean — hang up towel.
- Get dressed neatly.
- Put pajamas away.
- Brush hair.
- Pack backpack (including lunch).

Allow a fair amount of time, which is agreed upon by both parents and the child, for completion of the task. To begin with, this needs to be only a few minutes less than the child already takes (to ensure success). Set a time by which the set of tasks must be completed (for example, putting toys away in 10 minutes or being ready for school by 8:30 a.m.). A kitchen timer can be used for younger children and a clock will suffice for those who can easily read the time. Agree before the program starts as to the reward offered for successful completion. Appropriate rewards might include extra allowance, an extra nice snack for lunch, or being allowed to watch a special video.

Be very enthusiastic about the program, introducing it as a kind of game to motivate the child. Say "Ready, set, go" and start the timer. If the child "beats the clock," he gets the reward; if he doesn't make it in the allotted time, then he misses out on the reward. If he tried hard but did not complete in time, then the time allotted is insufficient (and he should receive a smaller reward for effort). If this is the case, try a slightly longer time next time, reducing it gradually once success is established.

Variations

Television Race

Television programs can also act as a kind of buzzer, for example, "I must get ready for school before I can watch morning cartoons."

Break My Record

Older children can enjoy simply being timed — trying to beat their own personal best.

See also:

- Past, Present, Future (p. 145)

❖ *Staircase to Success*   *Age: 6 years and up*

Aim
To set up a way of recording progress on a multistep program. The chart will then be used throughout therapy to record success.

Materials
Paper, pencil, and marking pens.

Method
With the child, draw a staircase. This can be cross-sectional or with a wide step at the bottom and smaller steps creating an illusion of height (see example, p. 50). On the top write "SUCCESS" or "YOU'VE DONE IT" and decorate it as the child wishes.

Create a hierarchy for the behavioral improvement with acceptable behavior at the top of the staircase and the present situation at the bottom. An example of such a hierarchy for eating a meal with no fuss might be:

- Eat all of my dinner most days
- Eat all of my dinner six times a week
- Eat all my dinner four times a week
- Eat all my dinner twice a week
- Eat all my dinner once a week

(Obviously, with eating problems it may be the size of the meal you are adjusting, not the number of completed meals, depending on the child's difficulty.)

Be sure to word what is acceptable as a *positive* behavior, and not as "not doing" something. The bottom step needs to be one which the child has already achieved so that it can be colored in during the session. The child then colors in each step as she reaches it. She can draw herself on the top with a winner's trophy in her hand when she reaches it.

Variation

Step by Step

The staircase can be used as a record of the exact progress to date on a sessional basis. At each session, write the child's progress so far on the next step. In this case, remember to start with a few steps, so that the child feels a sense of momentum, and add more as weeks go by to ensure no steps are left over, or draw them in pencil, going over them in marking pens as progress is made. Erase any surplus steps. When used in this way, it is important to have the ultimate goal written as a heading to the piece of work, for example, "I can sleep in my own bed."

See also:

- Past, Present, Future (p. 145)
- Zoro Reaches the Mountain Top (p. 44)

❖ *The Wall   Age: 7 years and up*

Aim
To help a child understand that his actions can create emotional barriers between himself and significant adults. This task is especially useful with behaviors such as telling lies or stealing.

Materials
Marking pens and paper. For the variations you will need toy bricks or modeling clay.

Method
Draw, or encourage the child to draw, his significant adult on the left hand side of the page and himself on the right. Make sure there is a gap in between. Explain that there is nothing to stop the drawn child and adult laughing and having fun together and listening to each other. Then ask the child what might stop that happening. Help him discuss the difficulties they are having, and at the end of this discussion draw in a brick for every difficulty (or category of difficulties) between the two figures (see example, p. 53). Put the bricks one on top of each other. If only one difficulty exists, make it a whole wall instead of bricks. Then explain to the child how these things make it more difficult for the caregiver and child to see each other clearly and trust each other. Talk about how this stops them having fun, or talking, and so on. Once the wall is drawn in, move to discuss ways to get over each difficulty, and as each "brick" is discussed, it can be crossed out (smashed, dissolved).

Do not leave the picture until you have discussed the way forward, crossing out the wall as you go. Fold the paper so that the wall does not show — this will automatically bring the figures closer together. Discuss this as the aim for working on the child's problems.

Variations

Brick Wall

For this variation, use toy bricks. Talk to the child in the same way, building a wall with the bricks as you go. When discussing solutions take the bricks away.

Over the Wall

Using modeling clay, make bricks as for "Brick Wall." A figure for the caregiver and for the child can also be made. When discussing the solutions, squash the bricks, and bring the figures together over the squashed bricks. Slightly remold the figures so that they hold hands or hug.

See also:

- Reasons Why (p. 25)
- Staircase to Success (p. 49)

Note: Following this exercise, it can be appropriate to do "First Steps Forward" (p. 105) or "The Conquering Soldier" (p. 94).

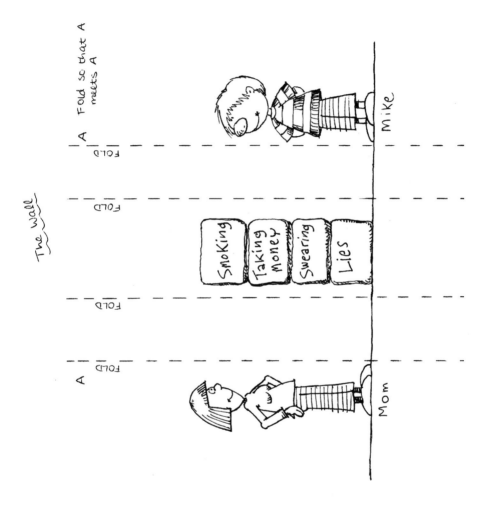

❖ *The Pit   Age: 11 years and up*

Aim
To help young people see that there are people who will help them when they feel they have no hope, but that they must act too.

Materials
Paper, marking pens, or colored pencils.

Method
Either ask the young person to draw, or draw yourself, a simple line which has a large U-shape in it. This depicts the cross section of a pit. Ask the young person where she sees herself, if she imagines the bottom of the pit is feeling as dreadful as anyone can, and the top of the pit is feeling fine. Draw, or ask her to draw a matchstick figure where she feels she is. Then draw at the top of the pit all the people who are helping her (that is, pulling her out of the pit). Draw a rope between these people, dangling into the pit just out of reach of the teenager. Talk to the young person about her need to reach out and take hold of that rope, and then translate the analogy into how she can help herself to make the best of the help offered. Make sure you do not leave the drawing until the figure in the pit is firmly grasping the rope.

The example is based on the experience of a fourteen-year-old girl who felt very alone and very stuck in behaviors which were causing her to be excluded from school, lose her friends and be in constant conflict with her parents. Doing this activity led on to a discussion about ways that she could make use of the help that was being offered to her. She was able to choose to accept some help (which included therapy sessions), while rejecting other help from people she saw as "interfering." Making the choice enabled her to feel that she was gradually taking control of finding her own way out of the pit.

As a review task, it is useful to return to this task near the end of therapy when, hopefully, the figure is drawn nearly out of the pit. The drawing can then be used to discuss how the young person arrived there and what must be done to prevent her falling into the pit again.

See also:
- First Steps Forward (p. 105)
- The Wall (p. 51)

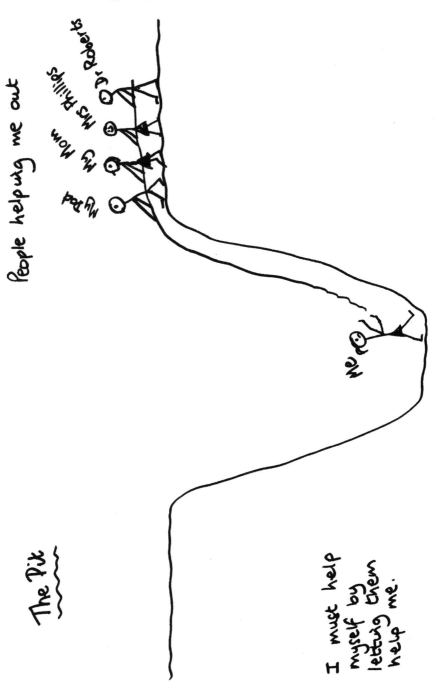

❖ Costs and Benefits   *Age: 10 years and up*

Aim
To allow the child to express all his motives for continuing a behavior and for not taking on different behaviors, and to help the child assess the possible advantages (and disadvantages) of changing behavior.

Materials
Paper and pens. This exercise also works well on an erasable board for older children (but needs to be transferred onto paper afterwards).

Method
Divide the page into two with a line and put the headings "COSTS" and "BENEFITS" or "ADVANTAGES" and "DISADVANTAGES" at the top of each section. Then along the other axis write the different optional behaviors, as chosen by the child — the problem behavior and one or more alternatives, such as "Continuing Skipping School" and "Attending School" (and possibly "Changing Schools"). Keep a limit on the number of options so that it does not become too complicated. Then, in each of the boxes, ask the child to write the appropriate pros and cons.

If this exercise is being used to motivate the child toward change, you may have to suggest some possible extra lines of thought in the pros and cons which will not have occurred to the child, such as longer term consequences, or consequences which may affect other areas of life such as relationships or lifestyle. Also, ask the child to write down his feelings about each option — fears and the comforts of familiarity are good to talk about.

Variations
What's It Worth?
If the equation for change appears close, the child may want to give each Cost and Benefit a score out of 10 for importance, and then add each Benefit up and subtract each Cost to come out with a final score (hopefully to enact change). This also allows you to see just how important each aspect is to the child.

Let's Work It Out
For younger children use only one behavior, for example, "Playing with Luke." Concentrate on the single aspect and list all the "good" things and "not good" things about it, then (if old enough) score them out of 10 in the same way.

See also:
- Future Profile (p. 103)
- Importance Jars (p. 133)
- Past, Present, Future (p. 145)

Costs and Benefits

	COSTS	BENEFITS
Not going back to School	Might not like my home tutor. I might be bored. I won't learn as much. I won't see my friends except after school. Can't do my best lessons. No after-school gym club.	I will be able to concentrate if I have home tutoring. Not with any nasty people.
Going back to School	Will have to put up with Lisa and her friends. Lisa is in my art class. I won't be able to concentrate in my exams because of Lisa.	See my friends. Learn more - do art and woodwork. Go to gym-club. Mom would be pleased.
Moving to the other school	There may be nasty people at my new school. I may lose some of my friends. I might not like the teachers.	Having a new start. Won't worry about Lisa and the others. Will make new friends. There's a gym club. Learn more than being at home.

Becoming Less Stressed

Many children with anxiety benefit from learning to reduce both physical stress and worrying thoughts. With these activities it is important to tailor the details to suit the needs of the child, to maximize impact. These activities can run alongside many other therapy aims and they can also help prepare the child for any more intensive work that needs to be done.

❖ Worry Box   Age: 5 to 12 years

Aim
To reduce fears and anxieties by helping the child to learn to set them aside.

Materials
A little box which the child can keep (see template in Appendix I, p. 155). A set of blank cards (approximately twelve, small enough to fit into the box) or slips of paper.

Method
Talk to the child about how we all have worries and that putting them away can help to get rid of them so that we can get on with life. Ask the child to decorate the box in a manner which she sees fit, and talk about where the box of worries can live. The box needs to be some distance away from the child to illustrate the point that she does not have to carry her worries with her. For example, they could be deep in a cupboard or in another room. If the child is worrying about matters that adults should be concerned about (for example, if her little brother is naughty), it

is appropriate to give the box each day to the caregiver when it is completed. This will illustrate to the child that it is the adults who should be carrying that responsibility.

Next, take the set of cards and ask the child about the worries she would like to put away. Write each worry down on a separate card or piece of paper. Then, ritually, have the child put the worries in the box, giving positive reasons why she need not be concerned about them. Now put the lid down. The child may like to seal the box with some tape or a ribbon. Finally, put the box away together in the place already discussed, or give it to the caregiver if the place is at home. The adult caregiver then has the responsibility of ensuring the box is put in the place the child has chosen.

Some children like to leave the box with the therapist. This can be useful if you plan to work on the worries with the child in the next session.

Variation

Free to Sleep

With sleepless children whose problem is caused by worrying, the caregiver may wish to use the box each night. The caregiver discusses the child's worries with her; they are written on cards, put in the box and, after reassuring the child about each worry, the caregiver takes them away. As the caregiver removes the box he asks the child to think of three good things to talk about in the morning.

See also:

- Clear Thinking (p. 92)
- Self-talk (p. 101)
- Reframes (p. 136)
- Spirals (p. 69)

❖ Old Rag Doll   Age: 6–10 years

Aim
To teach the difference between being tense and relaxed and to provide an easy reference for a child's set of relaxation exercises.

Materials
Project folder to put work in. Paper with holes punched, marking pens. If possible, a floppy rag doll, saggy teddy bear, or cloth puppet.

Method
Explain to the child that you are going to teach him about relaxation and that together you are going to make a book he can keep to help him. The first page will be about being relaxed and what that means. The rest of the book will be teaching him some exercises to do at home.

Preparation for Exercises
Talk to the child about the rag doll. Shake it about gently and watch how limp it is. Let the child draw the doll and above it write "An old rag doll is...." Use the child's words (if appropriate) to put adjectives all around the drawing (see example, p. 62). Some useful words might be "loose," "floppy," "saggy," "limp," "droopy." Add the word "relaxed," and both of you have a try at looking very relaxed like the old rag doll. If you have no visual aid, do this preparation through acting, but still make the picture with the adjectives.

The Exercises and Folder
Make a title page with "Relaxing like an old rag doll" and the child's name on it. Use writing which the child can color in later. All the rest of the work, including your preparation page, will go behind this title page. Next, use the text in the box, adapting it to the child's needs and vocabulary. Write the text clearly, spreading it out so that no more than one section goes on each page, and then you or the child can illustrate the text.

A rag doll is...

loose

saggy

floppy

limp

relaxed

Relaxing like an Old Rag Doll

First, wrinkle up your face
Keep it like that then...
gently let it go till you look like...
an old rag doll

Now shrug your shoulders up to your ears
Keep them like that then...
gently let them go till they feel like they belong to...
an old rag doll

Make your arms like a strong man act
(Show off those muscles!)
Keep them like that then...
gently let them go till they feel like they belong to...
an old rag doll

Take a deep breath to tighten up your chest
Keep it like that then...
gently let it go till it feels like it belongs to...
an old rag doll

Pull your tummy in to make it feel really tight
Keep it like that then...
gently let it go till it feels like it belongs to...
an old rag doll

Stretch out your legs till they feel really tight
Keep them like that then...
gently let them go till they feel like they belong to...
guess what?

AN OLD RAG DOLL

The basic exercises you will be teaching are a form of progressive muscle relaxation, scaled down to a child's level. They should be taught a little at a time, with a record being made of them as you go through. Do the exercises with the child as you come to each new muscle group. If you do this as you go along, the child will have more of an idea about what to draw. You will need to make sure the child tenses his muscles before relaxing but make sure he doesn't make them so tight that he is uncomfortable. Encourage him to hold the tension, think about it, then slowly let it go. Thinking about it is important so that he can, in the future, recognize when he is tense and use an appropriate relaxation exercise.

When all the exercises have been taught, relax the child using the text you have prepared together. The child may want to use them on someone else, such as Mom or Dad, before taking them home.

Do not forget to follow up this activity in subsequent sessions. Check that the child is using the relaxation exercises. If the child is old enough, he may wish to keep a record, giving marks out of 10 for how relaxed he feels, before and after relaxation (see the sample form "Relaxing" in Appendix III, p. 159).

See also:
- Through the Rainforest (p. 64)

❖ *Through the Rainforest*   *Age: 6 years and up*

Aim
To help a child become more relaxed through using visual imagery relaxation. To help her learn to relax by creating a tape recording with the child for her to use during and between sessions. This activity will probably take more than one session to prepare.

Materials
Pen and paper, tape recorder with microphone, and a 60-minute tape.

Method

Talk to the child about her favorite places and experiences. Steer her toward remembering the calming places where she felt happy — not amusement park roller coasters or "House of Horrors"! Add a few suggestions of your own. Alternatively produce your own list so that the child may choose the most appealing to her.

Example List

....

- My list of favorite places:
  rainforest, beach like in the book of holidays, grassy places.
- Other things I like:
  animals and birds, especially mice and monkeys.

Basically, your task is then to create, with the child, a very individual relaxation tape. At the beginning you will need to encourage the child to stretch and then go floppy. From then on it is a matter of helping her relax through her imagination. A sample text is given in the box, but it is important to be creative by adapting it to the child's likes and dislikes as well as making it age-appropriate. Be careful not to include anything that the child doesn't like, as this will sabotage any feelings of being relaxed.

Write it like a story, and include ideas the child has which are likely to help her relax; adapt those that are not. When you have written and agreed upon the text, it may be appropriate for an older child to read it to you very slowly to practice, ready for recording. With a younger child, or a less able or unconfident older child, you may have to record it yourself. Try to do this with the child present so that she feels it is her tape.

The text should be read very slowly onto the tape, the pace slightly faster at the beginning and end. Before the child uses the tape make sure she understands "relaxed" and "tense" by using words she knows like "loose" and "tight," and perhaps using a visual aid, like a rag doll or cloth puppet (see "Old Rag Doll," p. 61). Watch the child as she tenses her own arm muscles and then let her arm relax, to check she knows what she is doing.

Explain to her that when she listens to the tape she is to imagine that she really is in the rainforest. She will need to be thinking of real animals, real smells and noises, scenery and animals around about her, and so on.

The sample text is quite short. Try to gauge the length to suit the child. For a younger or very nervous child, it can help to make her feel more secure if she begins her journey with the therapist (as in the example, p. 67).

See also:

- Old Rag Doll (p. 61)

Text to be recorded (in this case, by the therapist)

We are going for a walk through the rainforest. Are you ready? It's time to put on your special sweatshirt — one arm up, stretch through the armhole, other arm up, and stretch again. Now feel how cozy and comfy the sweatshirt is and gently shake your arms as you settle into it. This is a very special sweatshirt which helps to protect you and make you feel very cozy and safe, but not too hot.
[Read the text more slowly now]
Let's walk gradually down the hill until we reach the trees. Listen carefully and you can hear the birds singing high in the branches above you... It is very peaceful in this place. The flowers look beautiful... and the sun is just coming through the trees and shining on them... You feel happy and content... You come out into a clearing where there is some grass and you see a little harvest mouse scurrying along. You sit down on the grass to watch the mouse... He stops to look at you and when you stretch out your hand he comes to you and you stroke him. The mouse has a lovely smooth coat and he loves you stroking him... After a while you put him down and then he moves away to carry on looking for his food. You get up and walk slowly along. The sun is shining and you can hear the ocean in the distance... Before long you find you are walking on golden sands and there are beautiful palm trees overhead... You lie down on the warm sand listening to the gentle sound of the ocean... You can hear the waves as they tumble onto the sand. You feel very rested and content... It feels as if you are floating on a cloud as you listen to the gentle sound of the waves. It is beautiful and peaceful and you feel really happy here... You float on the cloud across the land, over the green grass where you saw the mouse. You land gently by the rainforest... and find yourself walking easily back through it. A monkey swings lazily from branch to branch above you... What else do you see?... [Pause] What else do you hear in this special place? ... [Pause] Stop awhile and listen and watch the beautiful creatures of the rainforest.
[Resume more normal reading speed]
When you are ready come out of the forest back to where we began. Take off the special sweatshirt, stretching up one arm, then the other as you pull it over your head. Take a few deep, slow breaths and carry on feeling content and relaxed as you come out of the relaxation exercise.

❖ *A Me Calendar   Age: 6 years and up*

Aim

To help an anxious child know what is happening ahead of time and provide the opportunity to discuss it with his family.

Materials

Several sheets of paper (depending on how far ahead you need to go), tape or glue, ruler and pen or marking pens.

Method

Let the child draw his own smiling face and write his name in the top two inches of a sheet of paper (long side vertical). Draw a wide margin down one side of the page. Start to write down dates (with days) for the week (starting with a few days prior to the current date), helping the child to talk about "what's happening this week" as you go. Using the current week as an example, write down some of the things he has done so far and what he enjoyed and talk about looking forward to other events. Recruit the caregivers to help you fill in other items that are routine (for example, "Youth Club each Thursday"), and begin to stick other sheets of paper on the bottom as you go. Try to leave enough space for the child to illustrate events if he wishes. Encourage the caregivers to have the "Me Calendar" hung up at home, (perhaps on the back of the bedroom door), and review it regularly with the child. The child may want to put stars next to favorite forthcoming events and "T" for "Talk" next to any events about which he is worried. The caregiver needs to allot time to talk through the "T" events with him and reduce his concerns. When he is no longer worried about forthcoming events, encourage him to put a star over the "T."

Variation

Pleasure Planner

As part of the overall treatment, depressed adolescents may find it helpful to have a weekly planner where they put in at least one item a day to which they can look forward. To help them to be able to do this, prepare a list during the session. The list can include minor events and pleasures such as "Buy my favorite magazine" or "Take a bubble bath." Review progress in subsequent sessions, but make sure the young person really is planning ahead and has not just filled in the boxes ready for the session.

See also:
- First Steps Forward (p. 105)
- Future Profile (p. 103)

❖ *Spirals   Age: 9 years and up*

Aim
To help the child see how she becomes stressed and then to see how she can begin to reverse that process. This activity is useful to use with a cognitive behavioral approach to reducing anxiety.

Materials
Marking pens, two sheets of paper, pencil.

Method
Help the child draw two spirals on separate sheets of paper (see example, p. 72). As the spiral progresses, you will need to leave enough room to write between the curves. Head the first spiral "Becoming More Stressed" (or "anxious" or "worried," depending on the child's language). Begin to write from the *outside* of the spiral into the center. Use a recent incident the child has told you about where she lost confidence and become stressed. The text could be along the lines of "Was upset in school because teacher told the class off — I thought 'I am in trouble' and felt really bad, and that made me think 'I can't cope with going to French anymore' and I started to worry about other lessons — I thought 'I can't cope' and I felt really stressed."

Then take the second spiral and head it "Becoming Less Stressed." Start from the *center*. Write "I felt really stressed" in the center and then carry on writing, for example, "but I remembered that I have coped with a French lesson before and I can again. I thought about how I liked languages and looked forward to sitting with my friend. I thought again 'I can cope, I will cope' and I enjoyed the lesson."

On the outside end of each spiral write "STRESS FREE" and put arrows to show the direction the child went on the first spiral, and now needs to go on the second spiral. Discuss the two spirals with the child. Then take another "worry" situation and see if the child can turn a downward spiral into an upward spiral.

Variations

Heading for Freedom

If the spirals seem too complicated for the child, split the text up and put it in boxes with arrows going from one to another (in a similar way to "Escape Routes," p. 97). You will need to then do a positive diagram in the same way, but in the opposite direction. Write "WORRY FREE," or similar words, at the appropriate points.

Unwinding

This variation adapts the spirals for explaining about lies or stealing. Using examples of the negative consequences the child has experienced through telling lies or stealing, draw a spiral going inwards. For example, the text could be "Telling a lie can get you all tangled up until you feel like you are spinning out of control." Talk to the child about how she gets herself wound up in a web of deceit and needs to disentangle herself. On the outward spiral (starting from the center), write an appropriate text about the truth, such as "Telling the truth means facing reality and it takes courage and trust in yourself but it leaves you feeling honest and free." Talk about this second spiral in terms of unwinding and becoming untangled.

See also:

- Clear Thinking (p. 92)
- Practice makes Perfect (p. 75)
- Reframes (p. 136)
- Worry Box (p. 59)

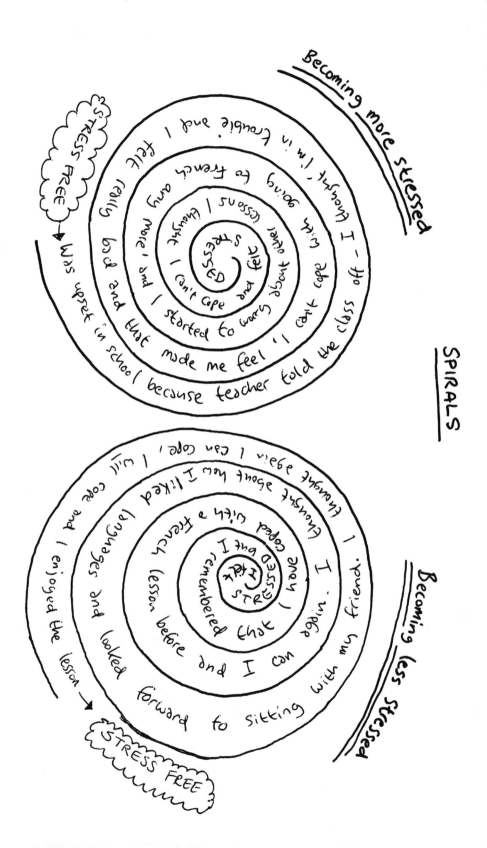

SPIRALS

Becoming more stressed

STRESS FREE

I felt STRESSED

I thought I can't cope and I felt more stressed and I started to worry about going to French lessons. I thought I can't cope with any other lessons — I thought I'm in trouble and I felt really bad and that made me feel I was upset in school because teacher told the class off

Becoming less stressed

STRESS FREE

I felt STRESSED but I remembered that I can have coped with a French lesson before and I looked forward to sitting with my friend. I thought about how I liked languages and I thought again I can cope! I will cope and I enjoyed the lesson

Learning New Skills

Many behavior problems are caused by a child's lack of skills in certain areas, such as socializing, and recognizing that the child has the ability to change family patterns. These activities reinforce the child's progress in learning new skills. All the activities are designed to be fun while teaching new ways of dealing with difficult situations.

❖ ## *I Can Help   Age: 3-13 years*

Aim
To instill a sense of responsibility in problem situations. To help a child change patterns of difficult behavior by introducing helpful behavior.

Materials
Paper, marking pens.

Method
Talk to the child and caregivers in order to identify the types of situations and happenings that lead to a problem behavior (that is, its antecedents). Teach the child to recognize these antecedents and help you to come up with some alternative strategies for how he could respond to those signals or triggers. Plan strategies for breaking the problem behavior pattern. Together, make up a star chart (or similar) for the child to monitor his progress, and title it "When... (trigger/signal happens), I can help by... (new strategy)." Have the parents or caregivers reward the child for sticking to the new plan; the

caregiver can also be encouraged to remind the child about it in the same manner, "You can help by...".

Some examples of "How I can help" might be:

- When Mom has to feed the baby, I can help by watching TV quietly.
- When Mom is putting away the groceries, I can help by folding the bags.
- When Mom is bathing my sister, I can help by laying out her pajamas.
- When Dad is on the phone, I can help by keeping Mom company.

Variation

My Responsibilities

For older children, a sense of full responsibility for a given task often makes them feel powerful and appreciated. Instead of helping out in such a way that they don't get in the way, they can become responsible for some aspect related to the problem situation. This works well when coupled with rewards. Make sure that the responsibility does not affect their relationships with other siblings or is not too great for their age.

Some examples of responsibility include:

- When we go out shopping, I'm in charge of checking that the TV is switched off before we go.
- When we are back from shopping, I'm in charge of making a cup of tea for Mom and me.
- When Mom is cooking dinner, I'm in charge of setting the table properly.

See also:

- Escape Routes (p. 97)

❖ *Practice Makes Perfect   Age: 3 years and up*

Aim

To increase a child's self-efficacy through learning to cope with difficult situations in a positive manner. Rehearsing the actual doing of the new, desired behavior enhances the chance of the child performing it.

Materials

Pen and paper. Puppets for the variation.

Method

When teaching a child to use a new skill in problem situations, she needs to *see* it, *talk* about it, and *do* it. Therefore, it is vital throughout this activity for the child to be actively involved in the development of positive alternative behaviors. While older children will enjoy this version of the activity, under-sixes will cope better with the variation.

Together, on a sheet of paper, write a list of "How to" for positive and appropriate behaviors relating to the problem, for example, "How to make phone calls without being embarrassed," or " How to deal with other children who push in line or bully." Help the child to understand that there is more than one way of dealing with a situation — depending on her age and development, she may also be able to understand how other people involved may be feeling.

Talk through what has been written down to make sure it includes all possible eventualities, such as, the phone ringing and an answering machine coming on, or someone reacting badly to a polite request. Work out how to deal with these situations, so that the child feels that, no matter what happens, there is always a solution at hand.

Practice the possible situations with you acting as the child first. This way, you can think aloud about *why* you are doing *what* you are doing, as well as modeling appropriate behavior. You should ask the child to give you feedback on how you are doing, or (if other people are involved) the child can pretend to be the person on the other end of the phone, or the bully. Rehearse this many times so that the child starts to learn the appropriate responses. The therapist should present a coping model rather than a mastery model. That is, if the therapist is *too* good, the child will think it is beyond her but if the therapist makes a few mistakes along the way but copes without being brilliant, the child is more likely to try. Add some humor if you can, to have as much fun as possible.

Now it is the turn of the child. Start by asking the child to pretend situations, with the therapist acting as the "other side," for example, the bully. Initially use easy situations so that the child gains in confidence early on. With each rehearsal, the therapist should be very careful to give about four *positive* comments to each constructive criticism, and make sure the same situation is rehearsed until it is confidently conducted. Then move on to the next possible scenario, until all are covered.

Finally, encourage the child to have some easy, real-life practice, such as phoning to the swimming pool to ask how much it costs for a child (something requiring one easy question), or ask Mom to pretend to be a bully pushing in line, so that the child gets to practice in a more realistic setting. Slowly, make the real-life practice more challenging.

Ask the child to keep a record of practice, for example, a star on a chart for every time she does it right. Maintain support until the child is confidently coping in the real world.

Variation

Puppet Practice

With younger children, the practice tends to have less theory and more practice of "rules" on how to deal with situations, which are easier for them to understand and adhere to. Use puppets to illustrate what happens when Miss Piggy throws a tantrum (for example, has to sit on the quiet chair), and after a few rehearsals with puppets ask the child "What must Miss Piggy do now?" and so on, so that the child can mentally rehearse in an active way.

See also:
- Escape Routes (p. 97)
- Spirals (p. 69)

❖ *Safety Hand   Age: 3 years and up*

Aim
To give children an easy way of remembering whom they should contact if they ever feel unsafe. This is a useful child protection exercise, or can be used with an over-anxious child.

Materials
Paper, marking pen, pen.

Method
Draw around the child's hand on a sheet of blank paper. Ask him to think of five grownups (adults) whom he can tell if ever anything terrible happens to him, or if he feels unsafe for any reason. Write the names of the people down the fingers of the drawn hand (see example, p. 79). For older children, the thumb can represent the immediate family. For children who are old enough, and know how to use the telephone, tell them to draw a ring on the finger, saying "This is who you will need to call." Add the phone numbers they need to the picture.

Ask the child, through repetition (this can be done in a fun way, such as interrupting a different exercise with "Hey, remind me — who is on your Safety Hand?"), to rote learn the five people and any phone numbers. Make sure he understands that if one person is either not available, won't listen or doesn't believe, then the child must move on to another and another until he finds someone who takes him seriously. Finally, stress to the child that the hand is always with him, to remind him whom he can talk to (if ever he needs to).

If the child has had difficulty learning the names of the people, encourage him to put the picture somewhere prominent at home. For a younger child, the caregiver may need to rehearse the learning at home.

Variation

Safety in Both Hands

For foster children who have contact with their parents, or for children whose parents are not living together, it is useful to draw both hands. Label one hand for each situation, for example, "At home" and "At Dad's." It doesn't matter if one person, such as the child's social worker, appears on both hands. Do not forget to put a ring on the finger of the person the child has to telephone, and add the number to the picture.

See also:

- Escape Routes (p. 97)
- I Remember Book (p. 109)
- Personal Pursuits (p. 83)

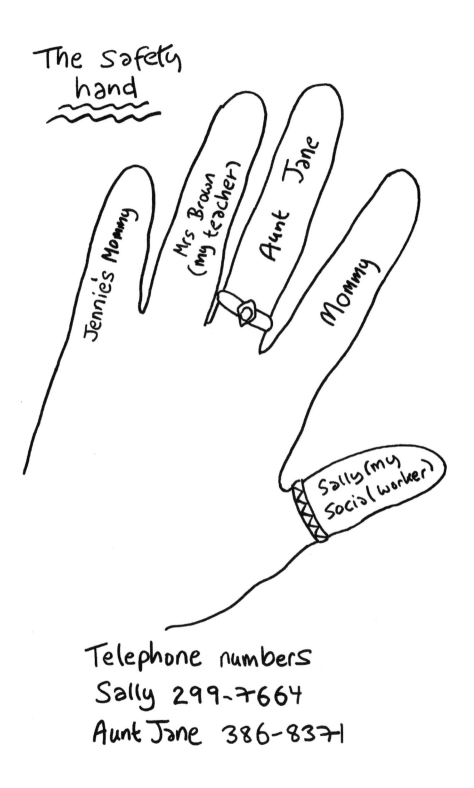

Shuddering Snakes and Likeable Ladders
Age: 4-11 years
❖ ▬▬▬▬▬▬▬▬▬▬▬▬▬▬▬▬▬▬▬▬▬▬▬▬▬▬▬

Aim
To help the child sort out behaviors into those which are acceptable and those which are unacceptable. The activity can also be used to encourage good social skills and to review subjects that have already been worked on in sessions.

Materials
A large sheet of construction paper, marking pens, dice and counters, possibly also a ruler.

Method
With the child, make a grid on a piece of paper as in the example, p. 82. As few as 30 squares will be sufficient. The START box should be in the bottom left hand corner and the FINISH or HOME box in the top right hand corner. *This is very important as it simply does not work the other way around!* Let the child draw snakes and ladders on the grid, being careful not to end the snakes where the ladders start or vice versa. At the bottom of each ladder write the behaviors you are trying to promote (for example, "Gave Mom a big hug") and at the top of the snakes put the unacceptable behaviors (such as, "Hit baby brother").

Game Rules
To play the game, use the same rules as conventional snakes and ladders, in which players move their pieces around the board in a "race" to reach the last (usually 100th) square. On the way, they encounter snakes (which return the piece to a lower number square), and ladders (which move the piece up to a higher number). The first player to land on the hundredth square wins the game.

Players progress along the squares in numerical order, advancing spaces according to a throw of the dice (or a single die, for a slower game). Landing on a square at the foot of a ladder automatically moves the piece up to the higher-numbered square at the top of the ladder — skipping the squares in between. Landing on the head of a snake automatically moves the piece down to the lower-numbered square at the tail of the snake.

The game ends when one player reaches the hundredth square exactly. A throw higher than the number needed to land on the last square requires the player to "back up" the difference. (For example, a piece on square 95 when the dice show 6 must move back to square 99.)

Take turns to shake the dice and move the piece according to the number shown. Each time someone lands on a snake or ladder, discuss the reason for moving up or down, making sure the child understands why the behaviors are there. (See the completed example of a game made with a six-year-old boy who was overcoming aggressive behavior, p. 82.)

Variation
Up and Down the City Road

Some children prefer to make a similar game on a larger scale with a grid as before but with roads up and down the board (put arrows on the road to show the direction). They may add in crashes (for example, "Temper tantrums") which slow them down to miss a turn, or achievements (such as, "Helped Dad") which give them an extra turn. For this game use toy cars, if possible, instead of counters.

The game can be adapted in many other ways to suit the interests of the child.

See also:
- Escape Routes (p. 97)
- Personal Pursuits (p. 83)
- Wordsearch (p. 87)

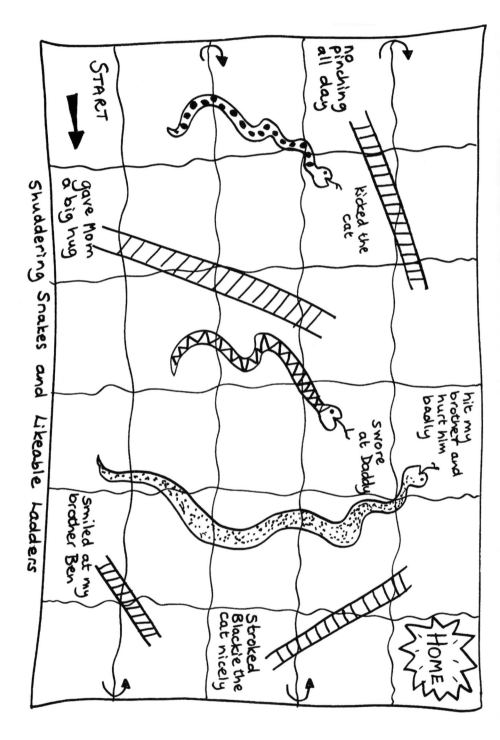

Shuddering Snakes and Likeable Ladders

❖ *Personal Pursuits   Age: 4 years and up*

Aim

To gain rapport, introduce topics, and reinforce new skills and standards in a fun way that also offers a nonthreatening atmosphere for discussion of difficult subjects. It can also be used to review and consolidate progress.

Materials

Marking pens, large sheet of construction paper, twelve pieces of cardstock approximately 3 inches square, counters, and dice.

Method

You can either have the board ready, or make it with the child.

Draw a long and winding road to cover your large sheet of paper, and break it up into squares. In a few squares write "Move up one" or "Extra turn." Add one each of "Move back one" and "Miss a turn." Add a large asterisk to every few squares, and draw in the "Start" and the "Finish"(see examples, p. 86).

Then make up a series of small cards (ten to twelve in number) which address the issue pertinent to the child (see the following examples). Make sure that there are more positive cards ("Move forward two," "Have an extra turn," and so on) than negative cards ("Miss a turn," "Move back one"). The cards should be placed in a pile on the gameboard/sheet. Let the child draw an asterisk on the back of each card like the one on the gameboard.

Using counters or small objects and dice, play Personal Pursuits. As each person lands on an asterisk, he must pick up a card and follow its instructions. Each card has a reason for the instruction (such as, "Counted to ten when angry — move up one") and this subject can be raised for more general discussion about coping skills/child's behavior. With a young child who cannot read the cards, it is possible to adjust the moves so that you always lose, if necessary, for the child's self-esteem. With readers, it is much harder and not recommended. However, praise the child for the way she has played, or the way she has been able to talk about her problem.

The game can be used to cover very many different topics by using fresh sets of cards, but it is best to stick to one theme at a time. The exception to this would be if the activity is used for reviewing overall progress near the end of the course of therapy.

Examples

Anxiety: Talked to Mom — Move up 2
Played with my sister — Move up 1
Cuddle with Dad — Move up 3
Didn't tell Mom about my bad dream — Back 2

School: Talked to Mom about what happened at school — Move up 3
Was quiet when asked — Move up 2
Did all my homework — Move up 4
Didn't tell teacher I was bullied — Move back 2

Toileting: Told Mom when I needed to go to the bathroom — Move up 4
No accidents all day — Move up 3
Forgot to go before we went shopping — Back 2

Variations

Personal Pursuits with Role-Play

For a group: more than two people can play, although this makes the game last longer, and is boring if there are too many players, as it takes too long for a child's turn to come around. The inclusion of role-plays on the cards can make it more interesting for working on topics such as social skills within a group.

The Game About Me

Personal Pursuits can be used with a younger child as a rapport-building exercise. If she is shy on a one-to-one basis, she will often end up enjoying playing the game with her caregivers, along with the therapist. Information gathered from the child about the activities she enjoys can be used for the items on the cards (see "My World," p. 17), but try to include some items which she does not enjoy, to create the cards which will move the players backwards.

See also:

- Shuddering Snakes and Likeable Ladders (p. 80)
- Wordsearch (p. 87)

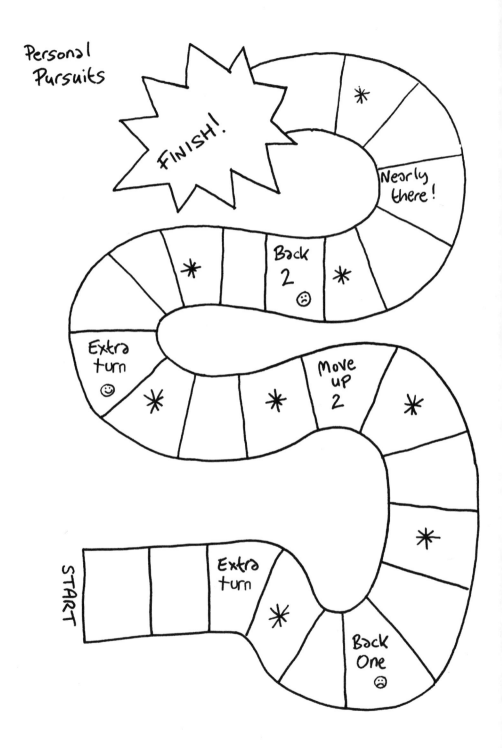

❖ *Wordsearch* *Age: 8 years and up*

Aim
To review progress through a particular session or to reinforce when a particular skill has been taught. This activity is only suitable for competent readers who are reasonably good at spelling.

Materials
Pens or pencils, two copies of the Wordsearch worksheet (see Appendix IV, p. 161).

Method
Use the Wordsearch worksheet provided. Give one to the child and keep one yourself. After filling in the top sections, explain that you are both going to make up a wordsearch where the other person has to find the words or phrases that will help him with his difficulty. For example, it may be "Ways to relax" *(read, have a bath, watch television, walk, cuddle with Mom)* or "How will Mom feel when I have stopped hitting my brother?" *(pleased, calm, happy, good, relieved, proud)*. Explain to the child that it's best to write the words first and then fill in with lots of spare letters. Encourage him to keep a list of words (but not show them to you) so that he knows if you've found them all. While he is making this, make the one you will ask him to solve. For younger children, make yours easy for them by using lots of Xs and Qs in the spare spaces.

Switch worksheets when you have completed both wordsearches. While he solves yours, you do the child's (he may prefer that you make a list without writing on his creation, so that someone else can solve it, maybe his mother). Do not panic if you cannot solve the wordsearch created by the child because of spelling idiosyncrasies or because he has made mistakes. Ask him for help! Discuss afterwards the words you both used and any others which would have been appropriate.

Variation

From Brainstorm to Wordsearch

This activity can work well with a group, and it is best used as a review task to consolidate learning. For example, choose a particular topic, such as "Dealing with anxiety" or "Coping with panics." Use a brainstorming exercise to put down on paper appropriate strategies. Put to one side the results from the brainstorming exercise. Ask each child to use ten words or phrases from the brainstorming to make a wordsearch, and then pass their worksheets to another child to solve. At the end of the wordsearch, the group leader can collect all the words used in the wordsearches and compare the list with the original brainstorming session.

See also:

- Personal Pursuits (p. 83)
- Shuddering Snakes and Likeable Ladders (p. 80)

Improving Coping Skills

These activities are designed to follow on from those introduced in the last chapter. They aim to provide a greater understanding of the child's own role in facilitating change. Included in this chapter are activities which will aid the child in problem solving. An integral part of this is extending the child's thoughts to include new ways of interpreting her world and looking forward to her future.

❖ The Battle Age: 6 years and up

Aim
To help the child realize that there are other people and other tools to help her when she is trying to conquer a problem. Especially useful as an aid toward reducing obsessive-compulsive behaviors.

Materials
Construction paper, coloring pens.

Method
Talk with the child about how there are people who will help her to conquer her problem, and how there are strategies she can use. Other things will work against her. Liken this to a battle, and encourage her to do a drawing with soldiers on either side (left and right). Make sure there are more on one side, say, three on the left and five on the right (see example, p. 91). The side with more soldiers is the helpful side, and each soldier will represent a strategy, technique, or person which is instrumental in facilitating the child's

progress. Some examples might be "Major Mom," "Chief Distraction Technique," "Corporal Coping Skills," "Lieutenant Remembering," "Private Relaxation." On the unhelpful side, put anything which holds the child back, for example, "Lieutenant Forgetting," "Corporal Lazy," and "Major Anxiety."

Let the child draw arrows, cannons, and other appropriate weapons between these two groups of soldiers. Make a separate list of each soldier that is on the child's side, and discuss with the child how best to use each one.

Our example is based on work with a nine-year-old boy with obsessive-compulsive disorder (OCD). It is a very useful way of working with children with extreme anxiety, who are often too worried to recognize that they have strategies and people to help them.

See also:

- The Conquering Soldier (p. 94)
- Zoro Reaches the Mountain Top (p. 44)

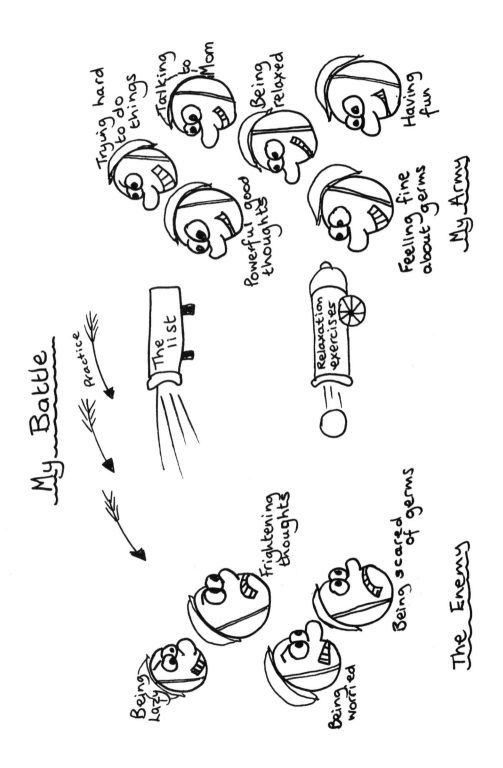

❖ *Clear Thinking   Age: 7-14 years*

Aim
This is a cognitive technique, designed to help the child sort out thoughts so he can recognize those which help and those which hinder. It should also help the child to practice positive thinking.

Materials
Marking pens and paper.

Method
Identify with the child any worrying thoughts, or those which contribute to low self-esteem. Once you have collected a few of these, draw two or three jagged shapes (see example, p. 93) with legs, arms and eyes, down the left-hand side of the page. These are the "Unhelpfuls" or "Pull-me-downs" so the child may enjoy making them look slightly menacing. Using the child's own experience, draw a speech bubble which contains the unhelpful thought, for example, "No one ever plays with me."

By the side of the "Unhelpfuls," put the "Helpfuls" or "Cheerfuls." These are more cloudlike creatures with friendly faces. Each Unhelpful thought needs at least one, and preferably two, Helpfuls to match it, for example, "Zoe played with me yesterday" and "They always play with me if I ask them." The child will probably need prompting at first to be able to generate helpful thoughts. Use the child's language whenever you can, and praise the child for any move toward coming up with positive thoughts. Talk about how the better thoughts need to start floating into the child's mind whenever unhelpful thoughts or worries arise.

For homework, draw a page of Helpfuls and ask the child to fill them in ready for the next session. When you review them, if they are really Unhelpful thoughts, then assist the child in turning them into helpful ones. Give stars to younger children for any positive thoughts.

Variation
Thought Columns
With older children, the same task can be done with two columns headed "Unhelpful thoughts" and "Helpful thoughts." Emphasize the need to generate more than one helpful thought whenever an unhelpful one occurs so that they gain practice in thinking positively. Older children may find this task easier if they imagine they are trying to help a friend with the same worrying thoughts as themselves.

See also:
- The Conquering Soldier (p. 94)
- Self-talk (p. 101)

❖ *The Conquering Soldier   Age: 8-12 years*

Aim
To help a child tackle a particular problem behavior by finding people and strategies that help her. To increase her motivation to change.

Materials
Paper, marking pens.

Method
To prepare for this activity, discuss with the child anything or anyone who helps her with her problem. The list may include strategies she has tried before, even if she has given up on them. Try to include anything you have already used, like reward charts. Make a list of these.

Next, draw one soldier alone (the child), taking up nearly a whole sheet of paper. It is best if this is a sort of Roman foot soldier, wearing a helmet and carrying a sword (see our example, p. 96). Now use your list to give names to the helmet, sword, shield, footwear and other parts of armor, such as the "Helmet of Helpfulness," "Sword of Speaking to Mom," "Boots for Believing You Can Do It," "Belt for Remembering Not to Talk Back," and so on. Try to use the child's own language. There's no need to spend too long thinking of witty phrases, but sometimes these come out of the discussion naturally.

When this is completed, encourage the child to take it home to put it up on the wall to remind her how to deal with the problem. Some children like to mark each item whenever they have remembered to use it.

The exercise can also be used to show a collection of strategies to address more complex problems, such as conduct disorder. In this case there may be a single strategy to address each specific difficulty. In our example, drawn by a fourteen-year-old, the difficulties included criminal damage, staying out late, stealing, doing no schoolwork, and lying. Part of the therapy was to begin to help her take responsibility for her behavior. Doing this task pulled together the various areas where she could begin to change and helped her begin to take control of her life. Notice how her mother was included in the plan so that she could take on a new role of helping rather than always punishing.

Variation
Safety Soldier
This can also be used as a child protection exercise. The child who has been abused can decorate her soldier with ways to protect herself, such as "Sandals to run," "Helmet to help me think get away," "Sword of screaming 'No!'"

See also:
- The Battle (p. 89)
- Escape Routes (p. 97)
- Safety Hand (p. 77)

The Conquering Soldier

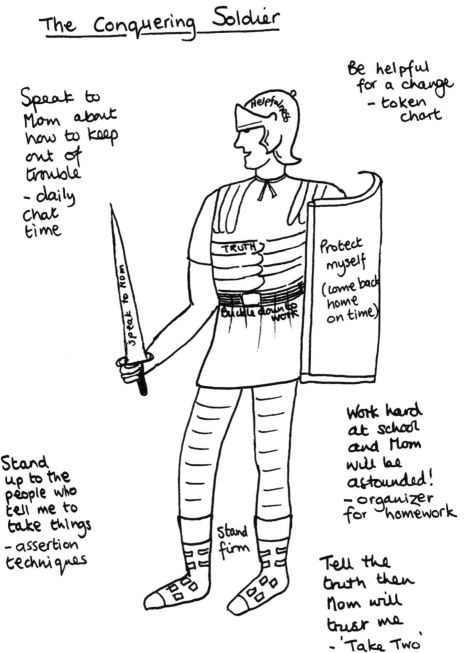

❖ *Escape Routes   Age: 8 years and up*

Aim

To demonstrate to a child that he is able to change a course of events by his own actions. This activity is particularly useful when a child is stuck in a behavior which causes others to be very angry.

Materials

A large sheet of paper, marking pens (at least two different colors).

Method

Collect information from the child and the adult about the event that has resulted in the child being in trouble or very upset. With the child, break this down into very small components, including his feelings and those of others. On a large piece of paper, write down the first component and put a box around it. Then put an arrow to the next component. Continue in this way with one event following another (see example, p. 100). Leave enough room around the edge to add further boxes later. Depending upon the age of the child or his particular interests, you can describe this as being a series of caves leading to disaster, or rooms leading down into a dungeon. Explain you are going to find ways out of the caves to come out into a safe area.

When you have put all the boxes leading from one to the other, you will have ended with the point where the child is in trouble. Make this a very obvious box with "TROUBLE" written in large letters inside it. The child may want to draw fire and dragons around this if they are really into the analogy.

Now draw a box which is labeled "ESCAPE" or "NO TROUBLE." The idea is to draw "safety ropes" or "escape routes" from danger points to safety.

Go back to the first box and follow events through to help the child to find places where he could have chosen a different way of behaving. Mark it with an asterisk, or make a door out of the box. Indicate on the drawing which color shows doors and which shows escape routes. This must be a different color from the one you used to draw the original boxes. (On the example given we have used dotted lines and different shapes.)

Ask the child at each point to suggest what he should do, and then discuss it. Only write down what would have genuinely helped him to keep out of trouble. Make as many places as possible for him to escape, but explain to him that the deeper he is into the dungeon, the more difficult it is. Have arrows going from all these suggestions to the box marked "ESCAPE" or "NO TROUBLE."

The example shows a typical situation which we often encounter in our work where a child does not want to do as he is told. His habit has become to argue, ignore, and then swear at his parents. Writing down the steps helps him to see that is how he reacts and how one thing leads to another. This gives him a reason to begin to experiment with different ways of reacting which can lead to new patterns of behavior.

Ask the child to explain the drawing to the caregiver and, if possible, you can explain that there may be other people who could have also acted differently to escape from the family pattern. If the caregivers are confident with this approach, ask them to use the exercise with the child between sessions. In future sessions, ask the child to describe times where he has used an escape route. He may want to write them down for you in the same way, showing how he has taken the good route and avoided the bad one.

When we have used this activity, we have been encouraged by the number of parents who recognize their own part in the problem and during subsequent sessions are able to tell us about "escape routes" they have used.

Variations

Escape to Safety

This can be used as a child protection exercise for a child to find ways to escape from difficult situations. However, if he tells you he didn't get away in time, remind him it's not his fault, but you want him to be safe if it ever happens again.

Family Escape Routes

The same activity can be used in a family therapy setting to look at how the whole family can change the pattern. Use a very large sheet of paper and different colors for each family member's escape routes.

See also:

- The Conquering Soldier (p. 94)
- Costs and Benefits (p. 56)
- Safety Hand (p. 77)
- Spirals (p. 69)

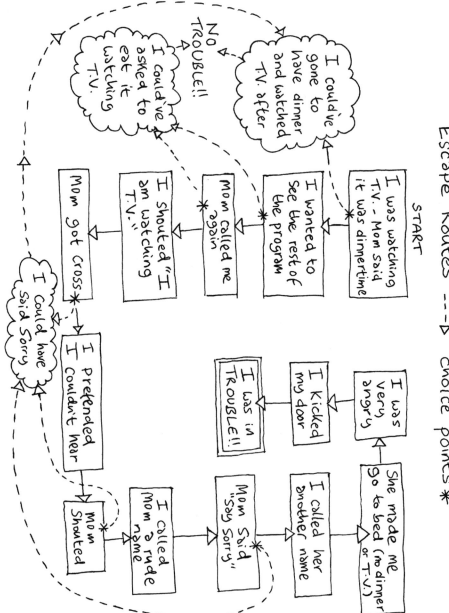

Escape Routes ---▷ choice points ✱

❖ *Self-Talk*　　*Age: 9 years and up*

Aim

To promote positive automatic thoughts in particular problem areas by helping the child to understand her thought patterns and rehearse positive statements.

Materials

Marking pens and paper. Strips of cardstock approximately one inch by three inches.

Method

Through your work with the child you will identify some areas where she is thinking in a negative way. Offer some scenarios to the child which are related to her problem area and ask her to track her thoughts — she may need some modeling to get the hang of this. Write these down one side of a sheet of paper, spaced well apart. The list should not be exhaustive because you will need to come up with a greater number of positive alternatives. Once the child has given you an indication of the sorts of thoughts she is having, you can group these together in clusters: for example, "lacks confidence," "lacks trust in others," "perfectionist," "lets other people's problems ruin the day." Under these new cluster headings phrased in words the child can understand, ask the child to think of as many positive "Self-talks" as possible. She may need a little prompting, but encourage her and use her language as much as possible.

Examples of positive self-talk include:

- I can love myself as much as I love...
- I am not perfect and we all make mistakes.
- I can accept myself when I make a mistake.
- I can forgive others when they make a mistake.
- I can learn from my mistakes.
- I can learn to trust people.
- I am able to try new things and take the risk of failure.
- I am a survivor.
- I will not let the turkeys get me down.
- I will achieve...
- I am loved and lovable.
- All bad runs are followed by a good one.
- I can do it.
- Count to ten and think again.

Write each of these down on separate pieces of card, small enough to fit into a wallet or purse. Ask the child to choose the five most important self-talks, which are relevant at the time, and suggest she keeps them somewhere close (ask her to decide where) so that she can read them for inspiration when the going gets tough. In future sessions, more self-talks may emerge and the cards kept close may need to be changed.

Variation

Daily Courage

If an older child is keeping a diary, she may be encouraged to come up with a positive self-talk each day which fits the happenings of that day.

See also:

- The Battle (p. 89)
- Clear Thinking (p. 92)
- The Conquering Soldier (p. 94)

❖ *Future Profile   Age: 10 years and up*

Aim

To help the child think of how things might be different in the future, and to realize that while change is inevitable, it can often be partly under one's own control. It can also help him to realize that to make change happen involves certain steps along the way, which can be broken down to small achievable goals.

Materials

Paper, ruler, pens.

Method

Draw a time line in one direction on a sheet of paper and a number of relevant areas of development down the other axis (see boxed list of possible topics, p. 104). Along the time line write approximate time zones, such as three months, six months, one year, two years, five years. Different time zones and different topics of development will be appropriate for each child. Ask the child to fill in the progress he feels will occur over the time span. He may want help in writing if he is young, or if he doesn't have the organizational skill required.

If the child tends to leap ahead with life, not planning the steps along the way, then start with the furthest time away and fill in the other areas later. If the child has not ventured to think about change, start with the nearest time zone and move forward, encouraging the child to think of how old he will be at each time point.

Once written down, review it with the child. Encourage him to tell you about his feelings on it, for example, which parts he thinks will be the most difficult and which he most looks forward to. This is an opportunity to "pep talk" the child on working toward a goal. It is particularly useful to follow this activity with "First Steps Forward" (see p. 105).

> ### *Possible areas for development:*
>
> - My friends
> - My education
> - Where I will be living
> - Earning money
> - Special relationships
> - Holidays
> - Hobbies
> - Having fun
> - My responsibilities
> - Major achievements
> - Things that will have changed
> - What will make me angry or sad?
> - What will make me happy?

Variations

My Child's Future

This exercise can also be used with parents of older children and adolescents to illustrate how parental views and child views are different. Discuss with them any discrepancies and how these may be resolved.

Future Spider

Alternatively, use one particular period of time, for example, five years ahead. This time frame can be used on a sheet of paper. Choose a time far enough ahead for there to have been some change in circumstances. For instance, a fourteen-year-old may wish to think about when he will have left home. Under the heading "How will my life be in five years' time?," make a spidergraph with the child's name in the middle and a topic as he projects it on each spider leg.

See also:
- First Steps Forward (p. 105)
- Past, Present, Future (p. 145)

❖ *First Steps Forward*   *Age: 10 years and up*

Aim
To help the young person see that she can work toward goals for the future by taking small steps toward them now. This activity works well following "Future Profile."

Materials
Paper, marking pens, pen, ruler.

Method
After discussing what the child wants in the future, ask her to head the paper "First Steps Forward," and divide the sheet into four columns. Head the first column "Future Goals" and the next three "Step 1," "Step 2," and "Step 3." Choose a few long-term goals where something the young person does now will make a difference. Write these in the first column, then discuss what she can do now. Break her reply down into very easy, relevant goals. For example, if the future goal is "Work as an engineer," the first three steps may be "Complete my technology project," "Catch up on my math homework," "Talk to my careers teacher about which other subjects are most important." These first steps set the goals to be achieved by the next session. Remember to review progress at the next session and as the sessions progress, pass the responsibility for thinking up next steps on to the young person.

Variation
Stairway to My Future
For older children (who can cope with more steps at one time), a long-term goal can be broken into all the requisite steps (task analyzed), and these can be drawn up into a "Staircase to Success" (see p. 49).

See also:
- Future Profile (p. 103)
- A Me Calendar (p. 68)

7

Coming To Terms With Loss

Children who are coming to terms with the death of a family member, friend, or even a pet, experience very real grief which may be expressed through behavior problems as well as depressed mood. This can also apply in cases of separation from parents or other significant people in the child's life. Just like adults, children can become stuck in their grief, and we have found these exercises usually help them to move forward. They will assist the child to accept his loss, have good memories and carry on with his life.

❖ **Best Memory Picture   Age: 3 years and up**

Aim
To assist the progression of grief through drawing/artwork.

Materials
Paper and pencils, marking pens, paint, crayons, or pictures and glue/tape.

Method
Ask the child what his best memory is of the person/pet who has died. Work out together how you could recreate this memory pictorially, and then do it, with the child being involved as much as possible. During the task or afterwards, discuss the picture to draw out the child's memory, using questions such as the following:

- Why is it the best memory?
- What else does it make you think about?
- What will you do with the picture?
- What would the person/pet think of the picture?
- What will other people think of the picture
  (does it matter)?

Include in the discussion any other topics that may arise from the picture, such as, what happens when someone dies.

Reinforce that although the person has died, the memories have not gone.

Variation

Many Memories

This can be used for not just the best memory, but as a collection of memories. This activity can be done with more than one person, for example, the family, so long as ground rules about respecting other people's memories are firmly established, and it is recognized that different people remember things in different ways.

See also:

- Forever Part of Me (p. 113)
- I Remember Book (p. 109)
- Memory Candle (p. 111)

❖ *I Remember Book   Age: 3 years and up*

Aim

To assist the progression of grief through working on the memory of times and events associated with the person/pet who has died.

Materials

Exercise book or special folder with pages, paper, and marking pens.

Method

Ask the child if she would like to write a special book about the person/pet who has died. First, on a loose sheet of paper, write down all the memories that the child has of the deceased. They don't have to be all good, although for this purpose, most of the memories are likely to be good, and the child probably wants to dwell on those. Depending on the child's age, you may want to write a little description of the person who has died, along with his favorite foods, baseball team, and so on, and you may write about what the child had in common with him, or what they didn't have in common. Then work out together which order these facts/memories should go in — they can be in chronological order, or sorted according to topic, or whatever suits the child. Write the book together, with the child doing as much on her own as possible (ensuring that the product is readable). She may like to include photos or illustrations, old tickets of places attended together, or other keepsakes. At the end of the book, include the fact that although the person/pet has died, memories can be kept alive.

Variation

A Book About...

This style of book writing can also be used to help in the grief associated with abuse, in that the child can benefit from writing about the good and the bad in someone whom she loved, but who abused her. Make sure the activity ends on a positive survivor note. An activity like "Good Things about Me" (p. 131) can be a useful follow-up activity.

See also:
- Best Memory Picture (p. 107)
- Forever Part of Me (p. 113)
- Memory Candle (p. 111)

❖ *Memory Candle   Age: 7 years and up*

Aim
To have a specific time when the child remembers the person who has died and has the opportunity to talk about her and grieve.

Materials
A candle which will burn for around 15 minutes. Have spare candles ready in case the child needs longer for the task. If you only have a large candle, make marks on it to indicate when it will be blown out.

Method
Introduce the task by talking about how people sometimes light candles in churches to remember someone who has died. Explain that when you light the candle, the child will be able to watch it burn, and it will be a special time to remember the person for whom the child is grieving. Light the candle and encourage the child to talk. He may avoid eye contact with you by concentrating on the candle. Have some questions handy to help the child if he becomes anxious, but do not be afraid of silence if the child appears to be able to cope with this. Ask the questions in a quiet, calm manner to aid the child's confidence and concentration. Some suitable questions might be:

- What color was her hair?
- Can you remember anywhere you went together?
- What is your best memory?
- Did she ever tell you a joke?
- Did she like animals?

If the child starts to cry, tell him that it is all right to be upset. See if, even while he is crying, he can remember a good thing. If the child becomes very anxious, uptight, or uncomfortable, ask if he would like the candle blown out, and if he says yes, extinguish it immediately. However, explain to the child that lots of people feel worried when they think about people who have died, but it is all right to think of them. Also tell the child how some people, even children, feel guilty when people die, even though it was not their fault and there was nothing they could have done.

As you end the activity, bring the child back to his everyday life and encourage him to tell you about something he is looking forward to. However, he may need a cuddle and a hug from his caregiver before he is ready to leave the subject.

See also:
- Best Memory Picture (p. 107)
- Forever Part of Me (p. 113)
- I Remember Book (p. 109)

❖ *Forever Part of Me   Age: 8 years and up*

Aim

As part of the grieving process, to help the child realize that the person who has died has left behind influences which have changed the child's life, and which will remain.

Materials

A large sheet of paper, marking pens.

Method

Write the name of the person who has died in the top left corner of the sheet of paper. Surround the name (filling the sheet except for the lower right corner) with things that describe her, such as her favorite things, what she was good at, what other people liked about her, her personality. Then ask the child which aspects of the person (from those written down) the child has enjoyed, and circle or color in those items. Discuss each as you go along. Then ask the child to draw herself in the lower right corner. When she has done this, draw lines or arrows from the chosen aspects to the drawing of the child. If appropriate, make each circle and line look like a large bunch of balloons held by the child (see example, p. 114). Alternatively, they could be described as strings which go to the child's heart (be led by the child). Talk about how the person will have influenced lots of people, and that these are the things that have influenced the child. These influences will last for the child's life, and thus, are forever a part of her.

Our example shows that the child likes roses, games shows, and gardening just like her aunt did. Other characteristics they had in common were long brown hair, saying funny things, and being friendly. We have found the task leads naturally to a discussion of other aspects of a child's life, which may be very different from those of the person who died. This makes it easy to leave the session on a positive note, looking forward to the future.

See also:
- I Remember Book (p. 109)
- Memory Candle (p. 111)

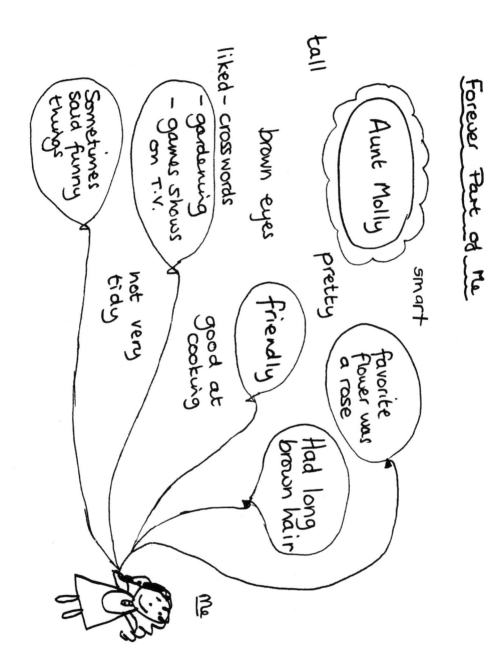

Understanding My Family

Families are such complicated systems that it is scarcely surprising that some children seem to be totally mystified by their parents. These exercises will help the therapist to understand the workings of the family, and also aid communication between family members. An underlying aim is to help each family member to look afresh at the skills and abilities within their family. The very act of the family working together should provide an opportunity for strengthening the family as a unit.

❖ Draw A Family (Doing Something Together) Age: 3-10 years

Aim
To establish rapport, provide an opportunity for the child to practice talking about himself and his family in a nonthreatening way, obtain information about the child, his family members and their respective roles.

Materials
Two sheets of paper, marking pens.

Method
Ask the child to make a drawing of the whole family doing something together. When the child has finished, ask the child to tell you what is happening in the picture. Write a caption on the picture or on another sheet of paper. Ask questions relating to the drawing to obtain further information on the family set-up and the

115

ways in which it operates. For example, if the child has drawn a family having a meal together, some questions might be: "Jenny is sitting next to Danny in your picture. Is Jenny always with Danny?" "In the picture you look cross. Do you feel cross?" "Daddy has a big smile. How do you feel when he smiles?" "You are all eating hamburgers. Who likes hamburgers best?" As the child answers, use the replies to write a short text about the picture as if written by the child, for example, "Jenny is sitting next to Danny because she likes sitting next to him. I look cross, but really I am looking to see who has the catsup. Daddy is smiling and that makes me feel happy. We all like hamburgers, but Mommy sometimes has chicken nuggets, so I don't think she likes hamburgers as much as I do." You may find it prudent to leave some of the child's statements off the text, especially if the child does not want you to write it down. However, be sure to include those in your clinic notes.

Before you finish this exercise ask the child if there is anything else to write about the picture. End on a happy note, leaving time to talk about something the child is looking forward to if this has been a difficult task for him.

Variations

Set the Scene

The use of drawings to obtain information on the child's perception of things can be used for different settings, such as his class at school, the child with his friends, the child in the hospital.

How I See It

In a family setting, all members of the family can be invited to draw a single picture or individual pictures about the same event. This can be a useful lead-in to discussing how different people see things in different ways or remember events in different ways.

See also:

- Family Questions (p. 124)
- Who's Who (p. 117)

❖ *Who's Who*   *Age: 3 years and up*

Aim
To help the child and therapist conceptualize the family. This is particularly useful for more complex family sets, such as where fostering or step-parents/siblings are involved.

Materials
A large sheet of paper or construction paper, marking pens. You may want to use photographs of everyone involved, particularly with younger children.

Method
Ask the child to help you to understand who is who in his family. Make a pictorial family tree showing all the people in the family. The child might find it easiest to work from a list of family members first, and he may wish to include pets, people who have died, distant relatives, and so on. This is considered acceptable as it is the child's perception of his family that you are interested in. The family tree should include people the child likes and those whom he does not like. The therapist may need to prompt by suggesting certain people to start with, especially if the family is complex — it needs to be stressed that more distant relatives can be included if he wants. If the child omits a whole section of the family, for example, stepsiblings, the therapist should note it, but prompt to have them included (unless the child states he does not want them, in which case you might draw a separate family tree for them), as they are more easily discussed when a part of the family tree. Once all members are listed, you can ask the child to describe each member and how he feels about them, as a start to discussion. The child may wish to include family feelings on the picture, as in the completed example, p. 118.

See also:
- Family Questions (p. 124)
- Heartstrings (p. 35)
- Portions of Parenting (p. 126)

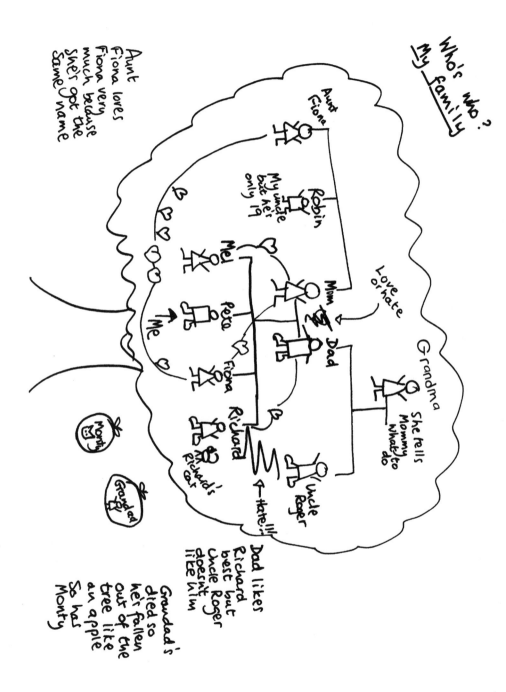

❖ *Family Rules   Age: 3 years and up*

Aim
To establish a core of family rules to which all members of the family feel committed.

Materials
Paper, pen. Can work well with an erasable board, but needs to be transferred to paper.

Method
Discuss the need for having a small number of family rules which assist the family in working together and helping each other out. Where older children (those over eight years) are involved, explain how family rules can be worded positively so that they are about "doing" rather than "not doing." However, younger children may need to have a rule that clearly states "No," for example, "No biting." Ask the family in general for some examples of what might be used as family rules, and give feedback on appropriateness, being sure to be positive about each member's contributions. Once the family seems to have the idea of what constitutes a positive family rule, make a heading on a large sheet of paper — "Family Rules." Ask each member of the family for one rule each, a rule that is fair and relevant to the family. Before writing each one down, obtain family consensus on the wording and meaning of it. If young children are present, they may wish to add a rule. If the one they say is inappropriate, help them be involved by suggesting a very general family rule with which the family would agree, and write it down as if it were the young child's suggestion. When writing down, be as specific as possible so that there can be no grey areas for the family to argue about later at home. Once you have a rule from everyone, ask if this is sufficient. Depending on the size of the family, the family may feel that they need another one or two, but keep rules to a limit of five or six. When younger children or illiterate parents are involved, try to offer a pictorial symbol of each rule. Once the rules have been

completed, put them on a jazzed up sheet of paper and present them to the family as a whole, as their rules. The family members may wish to sign their names under a statement such as, "We agree that these will be our family rules."

After this, but during the same session, see the caregivers on their own to discuss consequences of keeping the rules and of breaking them. Points to get across include making sure that the caregivers acknowledge to the children when the rules are being followed, and reward the children at times for this. When children break a rule, the caregivers should direct the child to the rules. However, if the child continues, the caregivers should negotiate a consequence which should not be *too* severe, but which makes the point. If a good reward system is in place, then failure to reach the reward will be a sufficient consequence on its own.

It is important that the therapist explains to the caregivers that rules do get broken from time to time, and it is not a catastrophe if and when it does happen, but can be seen as a fault of the program. For example, perhaps the rule is too strict, perhaps the child requires more supervision, or maybe the reward is inappropriate. Caregivers must also understand that the rules apply to them just as much as to the children.

Variation

Family Responsibilities

Instead of "Rules," a family can have "Responsibilities." This involves dishing out chores (and deciding who checks them) to each member of the family, to instill commitment to family teamwork. However, it is important not to have rival siblings checking each other's work.

See also:

- Beat the Bell (p. 47)
- 51 Ways to Praise (p. 121)

51 Ways To Praise
Age: 3 years and up, including adults

❖

Aim

To promote an emphasis on positive parenting and to increase skills at using verbal rewards. This can be especially useful when a family is trapped in a cycle of negative interaction, by illustrating that there are many ways of praising (it doesn't have to be repetitive) and many ways of making praise personal and enthusiastic.

Materials

Marking pens, large sheet of paper.

Method

Ask each member of the family to come up with as many ways of saying "well done" as possible, with an aim of 51. Write these down, either on one large sheet, or on many small sheets of paper which can be stuck together. Try to make it look interesting by circling various phrases, using different styles of writing, and using color. It will work best if you show enthusiasm, becoming animated with each new praise, and modeling it in an enthusiastic tone. The "Ways to Praise" can be taken home and pinned up in a prominent place to act as a reminder to all the family of the many ways in which verbal rewards can be given. Ask each member of the family to keep a note of how many times they have heard someone praise someone else in the family.

Fifty-one may seem like a lot, but for this reason can be a good number, providing the family members reach the goal and pleasantly surprise themselves. We came up with our own list (see the example, p. 123) which may help you with some prompts if the family becomes really stuck. Some families may be motivated to head for 101. If the family is not verbally skilled, the number may need to be reduced at the onset so that they are not disappointed — as few as ten can work. The list can then be added to at the beginning or end of subsequent sessions.

This exercise can work well with all family members if children are old enough (teenagers) to take some responsibility for providing positive feedback to caregivers.

Variation
Praise Record
For families who are having difficulty adopting positive verbal rewards, the "Ways to Praise" list can act as a cue where parents have to record which praise they use, when, and how often, with a goal of increasing the number of praises given within any hour/day/week.

See also
- Family Questions (p. 124)

51 Ways to Praise

Well done   GREAT   Fantastic

You're so smart!   Wonderful

I'm impressed   **Good for you**

You're a Star   You've made my day

Clever Girl/Boy   **I'm so proud of you**

BEAUTIFUL   That's my boy/girl!

I knew you could do it   You little darling

Brilliant!   You go to the top of the class

That's wonderful work

You're doing better than I am

That's Really Neat   *WOW*   Super

I'm really pleased with you

You deserve a prize   *What a great helper!*   terrific

FIRST-CLASS WORK

You've worked really hard

What a Sweetheart   A gold star for you

I love it when you do that

I think you're really good at...

That's incredible!   What an Achievement

I'm so Glad   Everyone will be proud of you

You must be really pleased   *EXCELLENT*

first-rate   marvelous

You've done really well   **out of this world**

That's sensational   SUPERB   *wonderful*

That's so creative   *splendid*   stupendous

far out   cool!   *AWESOME*

Family Questions
Age: 4 years and up, including adults
❖

Aim
To gain an understanding of family roles and systems in a non-threatening manner. This can be used with an individual child, parent with child, or with the whole family.

Materials
Prepared questions on individual cards. For the second variation, a hat from which questions can be drawn.

Method
Have a list of prepared questions relating to family life, each on a separate piece of card (for a sample of questions, see box on p. 125). The questions may need to be changed to suit the vocabulary of the child and the family circumstances, and some additional ones may be added which you know will be of relevance to the particular family. Ask each question and encourage the child to expand so that you gain insight into the workings of the family. End on a happy, fun question wherever possible, for example, "Who wears the silliest socks?"

Variations
Family Circles
With a family you can use circular questioning where each person's opinion is sought for each question (see Burnham [1986] for a description of this technique). Choose a fewer number of questions, as they will obviously take longer to answer. This can be an opportunity to recognize and accept that family members have different ideas about others in the family. Alternatively, it can be used as a task where the family members work toward agreement on each question. As you seek family consensus for each question, you will gain insight into family negotiation skills.

Sample Questions

- Who in your family reads the most?
- Who in your family likes animals the most?
- Who in your family makes you happy when you're sad?
- Who in your family gives the biggest hugs?
- Who in your family knows the most about cars?
- Who in your family has the most nightmares?
- Who in your family is the strongest?
- Who in your family gets up first in the morning?
- Who in your family tells the best jokes?
- Who in your family cares the most about hair styles?
- Who in your family does the most exercise?
- Who in your family brushes his teeth the longest?
- Who in your family keeps the neatest bedroom?
- Who in your family makes you laugh the most?
- Who in your family wears the silliest socks?
- Who in your family drinks the most soda?
- Who in your family bakes the best cakes?
- Who in your family gets angry the most?
- Who in your family wears the nicest clothes?
- Who in your family watches TV the most?
- Who in your family is the most ticklish?

If the Hat Fits

For individuals, the questions can be drawn out of a hat, with you and the child taking turns at picking one and answering if ice-breaking is needed. Encourage the child to answer the questions as well, even if it is your turn to answer a question. You can ask the child to make up some questions at the end. Remember not to give away too much of your own personal information when using this activity. If the child does not know the answers to some of the questions, he may want you to write them down, so that he can find out from his parents.

See also:

- Portions of Parenting (p. 126)
- Who's Who (p. 117)

❖ *Portions of Parenting   Age: 8 years and up*

Aim

To help children sort out the parenting responsibilities of appropriate adults in their lives. This can be especially useful for children who are in foster care or whose parents have separated.

Materials

Several sheets of paper and pens. For the first variation, boxes (see template in Appendix I, p. 155), or materials to make them (card stock, tape, or glue).

Method

Take a sheet of paper, and with the long side horizontal, ask the child to write "Which of my parents is responsible for...?" along the top. Define with the child any people who have a parenting role, such as foster parent, birth father, stepmother. Put the appropriate name at the top of a column (three parents = three columns). Explain to the child that different parents do different things for us or have contributed differently to how we are. It is as if they have a different portion (helping) of being a parent, just like eating a different portion of a pie or school meal. Then ask, "Who is responsible for...?" with the child writing the responsibility under the appropriate adult's name. If she does not understand "responsible," head the work "My parents," or whatever the child calls the parent figures. Adjust the wording of the portions to suit the heading, for example, "I look like her." Make sure the child understands that it doesn't matter if one person gets more things than another, because it is often like that in families. See the "Suggestions for Parenting Responsibilities" for some areas which could be covered (p. 127).

Attach additional pieces of paper to the bottom of the page if one column is growing rather long (otherwise the child may be tempted to put them in the other, more empty, columns).

With adolescents, adapt the language, for example, "Financial security," "My safety," or "Health needs." Categories like "Consent for medical procedures," or "My clothing allowance"

Suggestions for Parenting Responsibilities

- My looks
- My lunch money
- Buying me clothes
- Taking me places
- Making sure I'm healthy
- Giving birth to me
- Giving me a clean place to live
- Teaching me how to take care of myself
- Making my bed
- Cooking my meals
- Making me feel safe
- Telling me off
- Loving me
- Playing with me
- Helping me with my schoolwork
- Taking me out somewhere special
- Giving me an allowance
- Buying me food
- Listening to me
- Watching TV (playing on computer, making models) with me
- Teaching me how to behave

can be added. Do not add a section for the child herself. If she says she does some of the items herself, it needs to be explained that as she grows up she will naturally become more independent. However, this task is to look at the roles and responsibilities of her parents. If none of the parents are responsible now, you may wish to ask which one (or more) was responsible in the past. Indicate on the list by adding "used to."

Leave out items from the list for which no parent figure has ever been responsible. However, you may wish to keep a separate note for your clinical files in case it becomes relevant. If it is obvious that the child has important needs which are not being met, this may be something that needs discussion with the caregivers. Make sure the actual piece of work is kept confidential unless the child wishes her parents to see it.

Variations

Parenting Boxes

This method is better where a child is torn between two parents and likely to make the columns equal in length rather than admit that one parent has more of a role in her life. Make some boxes using the template in Appendix I (see p. 155). You will need one box for each parent figure. Label each box with the name used by the child for the parent. Write all the portions on pieces of card. Read them to the child and let her decide into which box they should go, letting the child place them in the boxes. After you have been through the list and added in any extras that the child has thought about, take the cards out of each box, writing them down so you have a list of each parent's responsibilities. Allow time to talk through the task with the child and help her to come to terms with anything that she finds difficult, for example, if one parent no longer has any interest in her schoolwork.

Parenting Pie

The portions can be portrayed as slices of pie or cake in a similar way to "Feelings Pie" (see p.32). Use a large piece of paper and draw a pie. Divide it into the number of slices you have for the list of responsibilities. Write all the items on the pie, then encourage the child to go through each one, coloring them with a different color according to whom the item relates. For example, the child may choose to color in blue the portions which relate to Dad, green for Mom, and pink for Foster Mom. Some portions may have several colors if more than one parent is responsible for the item. As before, do not use the version for a child who is obviously torn between parents or the resulting pie may have very even colors.

See also:
- Family Questions (p. 124)

Portions of Parenting

Mom

Gave birth to me
I look like her
Cooks me meals
Irons my clothes
Takes me to school
Looks after me when I am sick
Talks to me
Makes me feel safe
Reads to me
Buys my food
Buys my clothes
Packs my school lunch
Loves me

Dad

Made me be born
I look like him (a bit)
Gives me my allowance
Takes me out
Makes me cups of cocoa
Talks to me
Helps me with my homework
Buys my food
Bought my new shoes
Loves me

Paula

Cooks me meals
Irons my clothes
Talks to me
Shows me how to knit
Buys my food
Looks after me when I'm at Dad's
Likes me

Promoting Positive Self-Esteem

Children with poor self-esteem commonly fail at school and home. Other therapeutic approaches seem to get nowhere because the child has such a poor opinion of himself that he does not even think it is worth trying. He is probably expecting to fail again. Breaking into this negative pattern requires an approach that is nonthreatening and picks up on the smallest sign of any success. This will begin to reverse the child's opinion of himself to the point where other approaches will start to have a positive outcome. The great thing about helping a child to change his view of himself is the cumulative effect to be seen as he grows in confidence.

These exercises all involve the child himself, but work with the caregivers or whole family is usually required to prevent family patterns from sabotaging progress. The activities are not usually appropriate in cases involving severe depression or where there is an ongoing abusive situation.

Good Things About Me   Age: 4-12 years

Aim

To promote self-esteem and emphasize the positive aspects of the child. The task is also useful for building rapport.

Materials

Colored paper, marking pens or a pen.

Method

Let the child write his name at the top of the page. Then help him divide the rest of the page into six boxes. In each of the boxes write, or ask the child to write, aspects of the child's life, such as "At home," "At Dad's," "In school," "Soccer club," "Piano lessons," "My friends." Leave room in each box for at least one sentence. Then ask the child for one good thing about each of the aspects of his life. Help him to phrase each one in a way which emphasizes his positive attributes. For example, if he says, "Mom lets me go out if I've done the dishes," try to encourage him to write it down as "I'm sometimes very helpful cleaning up, so Mom is pleased and lets me go out."

When you have completed the written work, discuss with the child how he is unique in his achievements and abilities.

Variations

I Am A Winner

This activity can be simplified to create an exercise rather similar to "My World" (p. 17), but with an emphasis on positive attributes. If you have already used "My World" with the child, do not use this as well. If the child can write his name, ask him to do so somewhere on the sheet of paper (not too large); otherwise, you should write the name. Then ask the child about the things he can do, the things he likes, what he is good at, anything he likes about his appearance, and so on. Fill the page with all the things that are good about him. At the end talk about how many good things there are about him and how he is unique.

Passing on Positives

In a group setting, each child can write one good thing about each of the other children and pass them on to them, so that each child gets given a set of positive things about him — a great ego booster for all.

See also:
- Happy, Sad, Angry (p. 23)
- I Believe (p. 138)
- My World (p. 17)

❖ *Importance Jars   Age: 9 years and up*

Aim
To promote sharing of the child's values and perception of what is important in life. To build positive self-esteem. This is a good rapport builder.

Materials
Pen, paper, scissors, glue, and a photocopy of the worksheet list of items (see Appendix V, p. 163).

Method
Draw three jars on a piece of paper (see example), taking up most of the page. Put the headings "Not Important," "Important," and "Very Important" over the jars. Cut out the items from the worksheet (see Appendix V, p. 163), adding or omitting items as appropriate, and ask the child to paste them onto the jar that describes how she feels about each one. Make sure she understands that it is her opinion you are seeking, and that there is no right or wrong answer. It does not matter if one jar is full and another empty, just so long as she has put the items in the jar she thinks is right for her. When she has finished pasting, ask the child if she has any more items she thinks should go into the jars. If so, write them in the appropriate jar (or write on another piece of paper and let her paste them as before). Some items may need to go sideways to fit in. Once done, discuss the reasons for her choices. Emphasize how her responses are important and unique to her.

Variation
Importance Boxes
This variation is more suitable for children who tend to want to fill each category evenly. Make three boxes using the template in Appendix I (see p. 155). Label them with the same categories as the jars, then the child can cut out the items from the worksheet (see Appendix V, p. 163)

and place them in the appropriate box. You will need to write them down under the appropriate headings as you take them out of the boxes. Discuss the items as before.

See also:
- Future Profile (p. 103)
- Reframes (p. 136)
- Self-Talk (p. 101)

Importance Jars

❖ *Reframes   Age: 12 years and up*

Aim
To teach the cognitive skill of changing a negative thought into a more positive one. Designed to be taught once the child has recognized he has negative thoughts, for example, through keeping a diary.

Materials
A set of blank cards and pen. A black or dark blue pen and a silver or yellow pen.

Method
Illustrate to the child that there is more than one way of viewing a situation. One way would be to role-play a parent-teacher conference where the child has to imagine what is going through the mind of the teacher, the parent, and the child being discussed. Then discuss how one event might be interpreted in a number of ways, for example, someone in the lunch line pushes into you. This could mean:

    a) they were pushed;
    b) they are trying to push in;
    c) they lost their balance;
    d) they have a crush on you.

Continue on to establish that events can be interpreted in a good or a bad light, and that the child's own negative thoughts could be reinterpreted in a more positive light.

Taking the child's negative thoughts, from a diary or discussion, write each one on a card and frame it with the black or dark blue ("feeling down") pen. Stick to a maximum of six to eight initially. Ask the child to write on the back of each card one or more positive "reframes." He may need some assistance with this, but try to keep your input to a minimum. Frame these with a silver ("Every cloud has a silver lining") or yellow ("A bright idea") pen. In discussing each thought with the child, try to instill the idea that every problem can be seen as an opportunity waiting to be discovered.

For homework, give the child several blank cards and encourage him to "catch" his negative thoughts. Then he can write them down (one thought to a card) and find a reframe for the reverse side.

See also:
- Clear Thinking (p. 92)
- Self-talk (p. 101)

❖ I Believe   Age: 12 years and up

Aim

To help establish a child's identity and strengthen it. This is especially useful where children have lost sight of who they are, for example, through many moves in foster care following abuse, or the sudden death of a caregiver.

Materials

Paper, marking pens. Index cards for variation.

Method

A form of sentence completion where every sentence begins with "I believe…" The child may be able to initiate some of the sentences herself, but will probably require your prompts at some stage to suggest new areas to cover. See the box for some examples you could use.

Discuss the child's beliefs being sure to be nonjudgmental. Help her to understand that beliefs are what help to make her what she is, and that everyone has a different set of beliefs.

I believe …

- My strong points are…
- My areas of weakness are…
- Parents are…
- Families in general are…
- My family is…
- My brothers or sisters are…
- School is…
- The environment is…

- My religion is…
- My country is…
- Money is…
- Education is…
- Exercise is…
- Swearing is…
- Animals are…
- The future is…

Variation

Close Beliefs

For the child who needs to work hard on her sense of identity, complete the "I Believe" exercise with her, and then ask her which beliefs are the most important to her. Write each one on a card which she can take around with her or which she can stick up in a prominent place to strengthen her belief in herself.

See also:

- Best Achievements (p. 143)
- Future Profile (p. 103)
- Good Things About Me (p. 131)
- Importance Jars (p. 133)
- My World (p. 17)
- Sentence Completion (p. 22)
- The Story so Far (p. 148)

❖ *Permissions   Age: 12 years and up*

Aim
To reduce self-criticism and increase courage.

Materials
Paper, pen, and strips of card for the variation.

Method
Talk about self-criticism, how no one is perfect, and about having the courage to change. Talk about how giving ourselves permission to be the person we want to be, and to love ourselves, can help us. Discuss with the child which areas he feels he needs to work on, and together design a set of permissions. The box gives some examples.

Examples of permissions:

- It is OK to give my opinion in class.
- It is OK to make mistakes.
- There is nothing wrong with being top of my class.
- I deserve to be able to watch a special program once a week.
- It is OK to eat sweet things in moderation.

Write them down on paper and talk through each one so that the child understands the reasoning behind them, and hopefully starts to believe that he has the right to follow the permissions. Let the child take the permissions list home to read whenever he needs to remind himself.

Variation

Permission Power

Permissions can be written on strips of card, and carried around to provide strength when needed. The child may need reminders to look at them, such as a star or sticker on his pencil case or watch. Remember to make the memory aid fairly unobtrusive so that the child does not feel embarrassed if his friends see it.

See also:

- Future Profile (p. 103)
- Good Things About Me (p. 131)
- I Believe (p. 138)
- Reframes (p. 136)
- Self-talk (p. 101)

10

Reviewing Progress

As you come to the close of therapy with the child, it is important to go over the work you have done. However, going straight through each item could be very boring for the child and much more fun can be had by using a review exercise such as one of those included in this section. This will allow the therapist to review the changes that have occurred, and to pick up on any areas where more work is needed. Many other activities in this book can be adapted for review. The review marks the beginning of closure, so it is important that the child is praised for the progress made, and does not see the stopping of sessions as a punishment. Any long-term follow-up session should be set at this time.

❖ *Best Achievements   Age: 5 years and up*

Aim
To focus on and emphasize positive achievements to build self-esteem and confidence.

Materials
Paper, pens, adhesive stars.

Method
Ask the child to write her name in the center of the sheet of paper. Surround her name with her best achievements. If the child is likely to have difficulty thinking of her achievements, make a list of them first ("What I am good at," "Prizes I have won," "What I have learned in the sessions," "A time when the teacher has been

pleased with me," and so on), and then write them on the named sheet. The child can illustrate the poster if she wants. Follow this by discussing her achievements, making her feel confident and proud, and believing that her efforts can lead to good things. As you talk about each one, put a star next to it. Encourage the child and/or caregivers to put the poster up somewhere prominent at home, for example, on her bedroom wall.

Variation

I Am A Star

The "Best Achievements" (see p. 143) activity can be tied to a behavioral program and used as a way of emphasizing and celebrating progress and success, where each goal of the program can be added to the achievements poster. For example, "I can stay in my own bed after Mommy has come upstairs." "I can stay in my bed all night." With each step toward an achievement, she gains an extra star to stick onto her Best Achievements poster.

See also:

- I Believe (p. 138)
- Past, Present, Future (p. 145)
- Sentence Completion (p. 22)
- The Story so Far (p. 148)

❖ *Past, Present, Future*   *Age: 8 years and up*

Aim
To see the way the child has changed and will continue to change. To review progress made during the sessions.

Materials
Paper, pens.

Method
This is basically a simple pen and paper exercise which lists aspects of a child's life. Put the heading "My life" or, if it is already in a sectioned folder, put the work in that section.

Divide the paper into four columns. Do not put a heading over the first column, but label the other three "Past," "Present," "Future," or, if the child prefers, "Then," "Now," "Coming Soon." Take relevant aspects of the child's life, such as "How you behaved," and show him how to summarize this in the first column. Using that aspect, discuss how he has changed and fill in a sentence for the Past and Present columns. The third column should contain the child's realistic hopes and wishes. Possible aspects could include:

- My friends
- My behavior
- My education
- Having fun
- Getting angry
- Being happy
- My pocket money
- Living arrangements
- My favorite music
- My attitude to schoolwork
- My habits

Obviously, the aim is to help the child see that his life is improving, so try to have more items where he is succeeding than failing. If he is failing in some aspects, encourage him to decide on something positive for the third column. Some items may have deteriorated because of the child's developmental stage and it may be useful to point this out, for example a teenager may recognize that he used to be able to chat to his parents, but cannot do so now. Help him to realize that it is normal for the relationship to change as he becomes more independent. However, he can work toward a closer relationship as he moves into adulthood. Discuss ways of moving toward that aim.

Variation

Way of Life

For children who have demonstrated some artistic flair and can grasp analogies, the past, present, and future can be drawn as a pathway of life as it has been up until now, and then as a meadow for the future. They can fill the pathway with short descriptions of how things were and perhaps draw piles of stones for obstacles, with flowers or special places for nice surprises, and so on. The open meadow can be filled with plans for the future, with perhaps a rainbow over it for hopes and wishes (see example, p. 147).

Children are usually very encouraged by doing this activity and particularly enjoy filling in the meadow. If the child becomes very enthusiastic about the future, you may need to paste on more paper to include all of his ideas about life stretching out in front of him.

See also:

- Future Profile (p. 103)
- Past, Present, Future (p. 145)
- The Story So Far (p. 148)

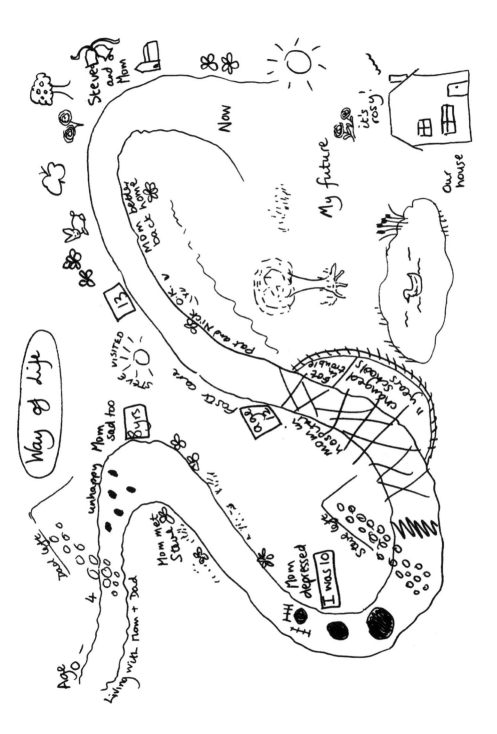

❖ *The Story So Far   Age: 8 years and up*

Aim

To have a record of losses and achievements. The variation to this task is especially useful for those who have had to deal with difficult life circumstances such as fostered or adopted children.

Materials

Project folder, paper, pens, paper, photos (if possible).

Method

Basically this activity is a pulling together of all the work done with the therapist. However, it can be combined with the variation.

A folder is made up by reviewing all the therapeutic work you have done with the child and putting it into story form. It is best done as therapy comes to its conclusion. Go back over any notes you have and any work which the child has done. With the child, make it into a light-hearted narrative, putting in what she has learned and how she has changed. Try to include some real incidents along the way which the child will remember, for example, if the child found it so difficult to behave in your room that you drew up "Rules of the room." If those rules have not been needed for some time, then that is progress and the child can write how proud she is now that she knows how to behave in the room.

This is a difficult activity to describe without the individual child's work, but a few golden rules are:

a) Keep it positive. If there are areas where the child has not made progress, put in ideas that will help her in the future.

b) If the child comes up with something unconnected, but which is still an achievement, include it anyway. She is still achieving even if it is in karate, soccer, or ballet.

c) Try to relate the progress she has made in the sessions to her everyday life, for example, "I learned how to control my temper better so I can be nicer to my little sister now, and Mom doesn't send me to my room so much."

d) Make it colorful and light-hearted.

e) You may wish to include a certificate of achievement at the end, perhaps worded "This is to certify that_____ has achieved the following: _____." Make it look formal by signing it and adding the date.

f) End on a positive note, looking toward the future.

Variation

My Life So Far

This activity will take several sessions. It is basically a Life Story Book, with the child making a record of significant events in her life and her feelings connected with them. It also focuses on who she is now. It takes the form of making a folder going through the child's life from conception. Include family trees, schools attended, house moves, moves to different families (if appropriate), holidays, hobbies, and so on. Let the child illustrate it and use photographs when possible of people and places. Do not rush it. Encourage the child to bring out the feelings associated with events at the time. You may wish to use some of the other activities in this book to explore particular issues, such as bereavement. *It is important that at the end of each session the child is left with a positive feeling about who she is now.* For example, you may wish to conclude with how the child handles difficult situations and emotions now, or with a self-esteem or identity task.

Do not feel bound to do the work for the folder in chronological order. It is less of an emotional load for the child if you move from difficult times to good times. If you put each little bit on a separate page, then pages can be placed in chronological order afterwards. There is also the advantage that the child can add to the folder if she remembers pieces of information at a later date.

Many children like to update "My Life So Far," so remember to give the child permission to add a record of important events or achievements which happen after the conclusion of sessions with you.

See also:
- Best Achievements (p. 143)
- Future Profile (p. 103)
- Good Things About Me (p. 131)
- I Remember Book (p. 109)
- My World (p. 17)
- Past, Present, Future (p. 145)
- Personal Pursuits (p. 83)
- Shuddering Snakes and Likeable Ladders (p. 80)

Appendices

Instructions for making a box

Enlarge the template to the size of an 8½" x 11" sheet of paper. Lay the template on thin card stock to draw the outline. Cut around the outer edge. Score lightly across all other lines ready to be folded. Fold into the box shape along the scored lines. Fold the flaps in and glue them inside the box.

If you are using the box to place strips of card, cut a narrow slot in the top.

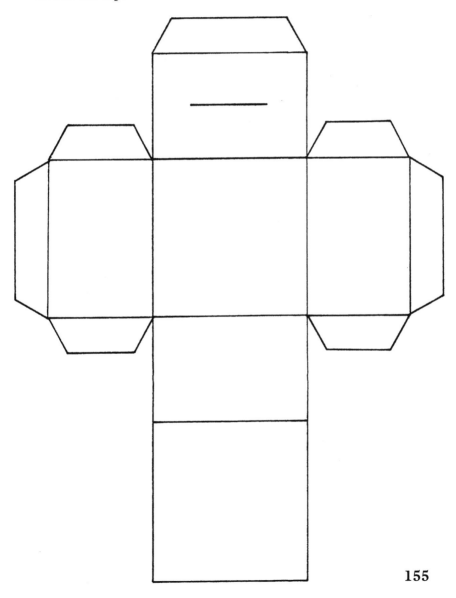

Name_____ Date_____

How have I felt over the past week?

	Not at all						**Very much so**
Happy	0	1	2	3	4	5	6
Friendly	0	1	2	3	4	5	6
Worried	0	1	2	3	4	5	6
Full of energy	0	1	2	3	4	5	6
Angry	0	1	2	3	4	5	6
Frightened	0	1	2	3	4	5	6
Upset	0	1	2	3	4	5	6
Lazy	0	1	2	3	4	5	6
Feel different from others	0	1	2	3	4	5	6
Confident	0	1	2	3	4	5	6

Appendix III: Relaxing

Name_____ Date_____

How do you feel before and after your relaxation exercises? Give yourself a score out of 10, with 10 being very relaxed and floppy, but 0 being very tense and tight. Don't forget you can use any of the numbers in-between if you feel a little bit relaxed or rather tense.

Very, very tense   **Very, very relaxed**

0 1 2 3 4 5 6 7 8 9 10

Date and time	Before	After

Name_____ Date_____

Here is a grid to make up your own wordsearch. Write your letters clearly in the boxes. Words can go up or down, sideways, backwards, or diagonally. If they are really long, or you have a phrase, then you can take it around a corner.

When you have written your words in, fill in the rest with other letters.

What is your wordsearch about?_____

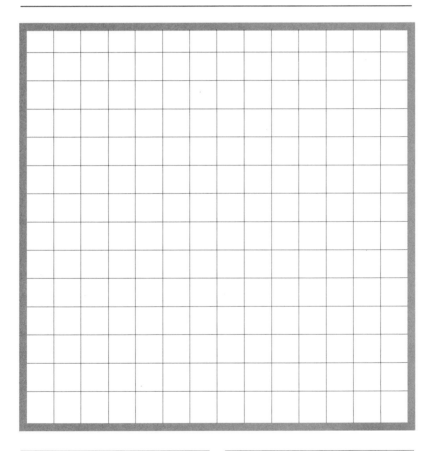

IMPORTANCE JARS

How important are the following to you? Cut them out and stick them in the right "jars" to show whether you think that they are "Very Important," "Important," or "Not Important."

- Enjoying yourself
- Being honest
- Having good manners
- Doing as you're told
- Having money
- Feeling peaceful
- Love
- Being happy
- Trusting people
- Growing up
- Feeling comfortable
- Excitement

- Being helpful
- Loving your parents
- Making choices for yourself
- Eating well
- Being smart
- Being healthy
- Enjoying yourself
- Being beautiful
- Being in control
- Working hard
- Having friends

References and Further Reading

Bloomquist, M.L. (1996). *Skills Training for Children with Behavior Disorders*. New York, Guilford Publications.

Burnham, J.B. (1986). *Family Therapy: First steps towards a systemic approach*. London: Routledge.
John Burnham's book introduces a range of concepts, skills, and applications. It deals with both the theory and practice of systemic family therapy.

Dwivedi, K.N. (Ed.) (1993). *Group Work with Children and Adolescents: A handbook*. London: Jessica Kingsley Publishers.
The subject matter of this book is widely covered by various authors. Theory and practice of group work are discussed when used to address a wide range of children's emotional and behavioral disorders.

Elliot, M. (1994) *Keeping Safe, 4th ed*. London: Hodder and Stoughton.
This a book written for parents about teaching children how to keep safe. It includes sound advice on protecting children from abuse, as well as covering other danger areas such as bullying, drugs, and AIDS.

Elliot, M. (1995) *Teenscape, 2nd ed*. London: Health Education Authority.
Subtitled *A personal safety program for teenagers,* this manual provides lessons to teach young people "good sense defense." Mainly for use in schools, it includes valuable information and resource lists as well as a script for a parents' meeting.

Fahlberg, V.I. (1994). *A Child's Journey Through Placement* (UK ed.). London: British Agencies for Adoption and Fostering.
Although *A Child's Journey Through Placement* has been written mainly for those working with children in care, it is of much wider interest to anyone working therapeutically with children. It contains much information about behavioral and emotional problems and how to help children to overcome them, including life story work.

Herbert, M. (1996). *Parent, Adolescent and Child Training Series (PACTS)*. Leicester: BPS Books.
There are twelve units in the PACTS series, designed for use in counseling clients and planning therapeutic programs. They cover a very wide range of children's problems and contain copyright-free handouts, questionnaires, checklists, and assessments.

Jongsma, A.E., Peterson, L.M., and McInnis, W.P. (1996). *The Child and Adolescent Psychotherapy Treatment Planner*. New York: John Wiley & Sons, Inc.

Kendall, P. (1991). *Child and Adolescent Therapy: Cognitive-behavioral procedures*. New York: The Guilford Press.
Drawn together under this title are contributions from clinical researchers about cognitive-behavioral techniques used to help children with many differing psychological difficulties. The book includes working with parents and special groups such as children with chronic illness.

King, N.J., Hamilton, D.I., and Ollendick, T.H. (1994). *Children's Phobias: A behavioral perspective*, New York: John Wiley & Sons.
This is a more specialized book dealing with fears and phobias in children. Covering both theory and clinical practice, it examines how phobias arise, as well as discusses assessment and treatment procedures.

Montgomery, B. (1988). *Getting on With Your Teenagers.* Melbourne: Lothian.
Designed for, and aimed at, parents, this book is also useful to the clinician. Using a cognitive-behavioral approach with conflict resolution skills clearly presented, the teenage years are explained and illustrated so that this period of development can be appreciated with humor.

Nemeroff, M.A., & Annunziata, J. (1990). *A Child's First Book About Play Therapy.* Washington, D.C.: American Psychological Association Books.

Reinecke, M., Dattillio, F.M., and Freeman, A. (1995). *Cognitive Therapy with Children and Adolescents: A casebook for clinical practice.* New York: Guilford Publications.

Sanders, M.R. (1992). *Every Parent: A positive approach to children's behavior.* Reading, MA: Addison-Wesley Publishing Company.
This book, written for parents, covers a wide range of children's common problems from infancy to late preschool years. It provides a positive behavioral approach which is very easy to understand and follow. It offers many practical ideas to promote positive management, with functional analysis and program planning explained at the end of the book.

Webster-Stratton, C. (1992). *The Incredible Years.* Toronto: Umbrella Press.
Written to assist parents of 3- to 8-year-olds, this book is packed with chapters covering the essentials of positive behavior management and common behavioral programs. It explains the importance of praise, limit-setting, how to play with your child, as well as offering substantial information and advice on effective communication and problem-solving.

Subject Index

Activities Index

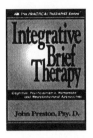